T0095451

Delicious Rejection

The Memoirs of a Hopeless Romantic

By

James Robert Russell

iUniverse, Inc.

New York   Bloomington

iUniverse books may be ordered through booksellers or by contacting:

iUniverse
1663 Liberty Drive
Bloomington, IN 47403
www.iuniverse.com
1-800-Authors (1-800-288-4677)

Because of the dynamic nature of the Internet, any Web addresses or links contained in this book may have changed since publication and may no longer be valid. The views expressed in this work are solely those of the author and do not necessarily reflect the views of the publisher, and the publisher hereby disclaims any responsibility for them.

ISBN: 978-1-4502-4333-9 (sc)
ISBN: 978-1-4502-4335-3 (hc)
ISBN: 978-1-4502-4334-6 (ebook)

Printed in the United States of America

iUniverse rev. date: 07/23/2010

# Table of Contents

# DEDICATION

This book is dedicated to all the women I've been blessed to know and love. It has been written as a tribute to the intelligence, beauty, and charm that all of you possess. Whether you are mentioned individually or not, please know that your influence has shaped the person that I have become. I cherish all the memories; still feel the pain. By sharing our lives, I hope that it will give others hope that they too can find or keep love. Maybe show them that it's not too late to make some wonderful memories; to experience the kaleido-scope of emotions that is love.

# ACKNOWLEDGEMENT

To the many people that either helped or encouraged me during this project, I give my heartfelt thanks. I truly appreciate the time and emotion expended to help me fulfill my dream. Specifically, I would like to mention my mother Vivian, my daughter Deanna, and friends Carolyn, Marjorie, Susan, Pamela, and John. Thank you.

My heartfelt thanks to my sons for their creativity, Jonathan for the cover art and Jason for my website deliciousrejection.com

# INTRODUCTION

For those of you expecting to read a scandalous tell all expose, written to embarrass and humiliate the subjects of these stories; you have picked the wrong book. However, if you enjoy romance; the joys and pain of human interaction, recounted by someone that loves and respects; then you're in for the ride of your life. Some of these stories are well, racy to put it mildly. Some details are purposely left out to leave something to the imagination, feel free to let your imagination run free because frankly, it's probably close to being correct. We've had some good times!! However, the real names in some of explicit personal stuff were left out to keep from embarrassing the ladies. Let's be fair they've all moved on, and a gentleman never tells. I can only hope to do the ladies justice on paper. To adequately express the love, happiness, pain and depth of the relationships we've shared. To paint the vivid personalities they possess. To express the contents of my soul, heart, and mind. Read it with your eyes; picture it in your mind's eye. Let it touch your heart, tease, please and excite you. Feel the pain in your gut, the strain on your mind. Let it bring a smile to your face, maybe a tear to your eyes. For this is the story of my life. That is the point isn't? To live, experience and relish life. Enjoy!

# Chapter One

## The Early Years

I was born a predominately black child and grew up in a predominately black neighborhood. This situation has certain unspoken responsibilities, inherent expectations. In retrospect, I probably failed in most of those requirements. Fortunately, I've never measured my success or worth by other's standards. I was skinny, freakishly tall with abnormally large ears which took years to grow into. Possessing above average athleticism, I was able to compete with my peers despite deficiencies in coordination, aggression and toughness. On the positive side of the ledger I was intelligent, creative and passionate about everything. Accepted in both my own peer group and by older kids; I was given two nicknames in addition to the one given to me by my family. The first was Dumbo; a not so subtle reference to the size of my ears. The latter was Computer. A flattering tribute to my amazing math acuity; keep in mind this was the early sixties and computers though primitive by today's standard were a marvel at the time.

The fairer sex has always been of interest to me; even before I was old enough to know why. In the early sixties there was still a great deal of formality. Trips to shop downtown were my favorite, especially at Christmas time. Men traditionally wore suits. Women always wore dresses; accessorized by hats and gloves. Heels and hose were an absolute necessity. This fact was not lost on me. I guess I've always been a leg man. The versatility of women has always fascinated me. Housewives transformed themselves into models for PTA meetings; the isles of the auditorium their runways.

My sensitivity was apparent very early in my formative years. There was a local children's TV show hosted by Miss Barbara. The show ended with Miss Barbara singing a song which included her looking through a hoop and pretending to see her fans; calling out their names individually. "I see Billy and Susan etc". Confident that she was speaking directly to me, I didn't rest until I was a guest on the show. On the other side of the coin, there was a song on another of my favorite shows that even now on a bad day will recall pain. I suppose that there has always been a part of me that never felt like it belonged or fit in. At five years old the sadness was uncontrollable. The chorus of the song; "I'm a lonely little petunia in an onion patch, an onion patch, an onion patch. I'm a lonely little petunia in an onion patch; and all I do is cry all day" unleashed torrents of tears.

Of all of the holidays that we celebrated in elementary school; Valentine's Day was by far my favorite. It was my opportunity to express my feelings to those few special girls in my class. More importantly, gauge their opinions of me. These were the times before political correctness became a part of curriculum. We were allowed to give cards to the kids we chose to without concern for the feelings of those who might get fewer cards than others. Therefore, it could be stressful on many levels. But I believe this is a necessary part of the maturation process.

My family wasn't well off, but we were creative. Buying Valentine's Day cards was not in the budget; so we made them from construction paper and lace doilies. It was tough even then for kids to be individuals in school. I think the fact that I was almost always, well "different" made me tougher. I learned to set the trend for others to follow. Actually, I thought the homemade touch made my cards special. At the advice of my mother, I gave cards to all of the girls in the class. Later when I had my own money; earned on my paper route, I added candy. However, there were two sizes of cards; the special girls, the ones I felt attracted to got larger ones. Unfortunately, they also attracted the lion's share of the attention from the rest of the boys in the class. I never got the level of attention that I wanted from them though I remained friends with most of them through high school.

I was flattered when at my twentieth high school reunion one of the "special girls" that had moved away, but married one of my classmates came up to me and told me she had kept a Valentine that I had given her saying, "it had meant a lot to her". The only other direct reaction I received was in the fifth grade. I was walking home from school in front of a group of "older" girls, sixth graders actually. When one of them who lived on my street invited me to walk with them I was excited, but as soon as I reached the group she slapped me as hard as I had ever been hit to date. She had been given a smaller card than her friend. My feelings were hurt even though she had never really paid any attention to me in the past. As I grew in age and experience, I realized that slap in "girl speak" meant that she liked me more than she ever let on, and she felt slighted by the smaller card. She never spoke to me again.

The "special" girls had "beautiful" qualities even at that age. They were usually taller; always prettier, better dressed, smarter, musically or artistically gifted, more refined and mature than the rest of the girls in the class. They even had better handwriting. They shaped my definition of "beautiful" at an early age. They raised the level of the everyday activity to an art form. I was enchanted. It seemed as though the gods were always smiling on them. One of them had an unfortunate bicycle accident on my street while visiting her grandmother. It could have been very serious, as she hit the car broadside. The impact caused her to fly over the handlebars and across the hood of the car. Fortunately, the only injury she sustained was a small "V" shaped cut on the upper thigh of her otherwise flawless legs. The resulting scar was only slightly darker than her skin tone and was placed such that you would have to be intimate with her to see it. It couldn't have been more delicate if it had been tattooed on. Her first name began with a "V"; Beautiful.

I didn't know it at the time but my lifelong experiences with the opposite sex could be summed up by two encounters in my adolescence, the formative years. On one hand the flair for the dramatic. On the other: despair, disappointment, and rejection.

# Chapter Two

## First Kiss

It was a hot day, more than one hundred degrees in the shade, if there was any to be found. We climbed the winding red clay steps to an unknown destination. It was the second day of a journey that frankly was a miracle come true. As we reached the summit and gazed upon the incredible scenery for the first time our silence spoke volumes about the amazing view.

The summit was actually a garden on top of a mesa. It was a simple place with stones encircling smoothly raked red dirt. The stone benches arranged on the edges provided a ringside seat to the probably endless battle of the sea versus sky for the title of bluest in nature. The battle, officiated by the rocky shore was fueled and orchestrated by the wind. It provided each with a contrast to measure the incredibly vivid blues. To the sea, the wind gave white caps and foam rolling in on wave after wave from the Isle of Goree in the distance. The wind's gifts to the sky were the constantly changing shape of wispy clouds that sped by.

It was hard to believe that as a boy of nearly thirteen I was seeing the Atlantic Ocean for the first time, from the other side no less. It was nineteen sixty-nine. The height of the Black Power movement and I was in Dakar, Senegal. I was tall for my age at five feet seven, but thin at 116 pounds. The scenery had so overwhelmed me that I had forgotten that I was still holding Sheila's hand. We had gravitated towards each other on the long flight from New York. It was an unlikely alliance. She was my age, but light years ahead of me socially. She wore green shorts, tennis shoes and a white sleeveless blouse. She was built similarly to me, but in three-quarter scale. The wind had rearranged her long bangs to resemble rearing horses. The benefit was that I saw her mellow brown eyes for the first time in the light of the sun.

She walked to the edge to get a better view of the boulder strewn shore. I nervously followed her just in time to reach for her slender waist, as a strong gust of wind unsteadied her stance. She turned to face me smiling. I had both hands on her thin, but curvy hips now. This was the first time I had actually held a girl in that manner. I stood frozen, inexperienced and overwhelmed. We stood for what seemed like an hour and it felt like a dream. Her warm but confident voice awakened me with the single word, "kiss" as she stepped into my arms, stood on her tiptoes and kissed me.

To this day I don't remember climbing back down the stairs or walking her back to the hotel. My first recollection was being let back into my hotel room by my roommates and lifelong friends. I couldn't find the key that was secure in my pocket. Upon entering, I was asked, "Where I had been?" "Why I had missed lunch?" I blurted out "I kissed Sheila" to the surprise and amazement of my friends. I stood there motionless in a hailstorm of questions. I only answered one of them. "How was it?" My response? "As smooth as silk."

# Chapter Three

## Call Waiting

This story is probably the basis of my entire social interaction with the fairer sex. It provided me with an operational principle that I still use today. More information on that subject will be provided later. Upon reflection, I am confronted with the source of my extreme level of patience, tolerance for emotional pain and then forgiveness.

The title "Call Waiting" may be slightly deceiving. The term is a contemporary one, but the setting of this story is the late '60s. The telephone at that time was almost a "luxury" appliance in my neighborhood. We had ourselves just recently "upgraded" to a private line. Previously, we could only afford a "party line" which you shared with up to three other families. Access was obviously limited, and privacy was certainly not a guarantee. But it served the purpose. The phone we chose was a single black rotary dial model with a long cord. White and beige (decorator colors) were available at extra cost. There was not a phone on the second level of our home. They were called extensions. They were available with or without a dial. Why not? I already explained. It cost extra. Operation was simple. When you called someone and they didn't answer they were either not home or ignoring the phone. So you called back later. If you got the busy signal, they were on the phone and therefore home, so you called back later. The final and most important thing was this. As a child you didn't touch the phone unless instructed. Usually this honor was granted by a parent to tell whoever was on the line that your parents weren't home. Think of it as sort of a primitive form of call screening. You didn't answer the phone because it wasn't for you. You didn't talk on the phone to your friends "tying up" the line because whatever you wanted to say wasn't important and should have been said before you left school. It could certainly wait until tomorrow.

You dare not use the excuse that you needed to get a homework assignment because you should have been paying attention in school. Anyone born after 1970 won't believe this. Those born before 1960 are probably smiling. It was against that backdrop that this saga takes place.

I was thirteen and in Jr. High school. I had only recently explored my emerging interest is girls. My first kiss had been earlier that summer. The object of my youthful desire this time was Candace. She was very intelligent. We were both in advanced studies, she in Section 1 and I in Section 2. We had some of our classes together. Yes, tracking was legal then, and might I say productive. She was attractive and tall, almost my height of five-foot seven. She had "good hair", was light skinned and came from a better neighborhood. In retrospect, she was beyond my reach for several reasons.

We became friendly as the fall semester progressed. I helped her in Geometry, she tutored me in English. One day during lunch period she struck up a conversation. This was major, as she had to leave her girlfriends and venture over to our boys' table. This act alone gained me serious status points among my friends. Suddenly, the bell rang signaling the end of our half of the lunch period. She asked me for my phone number to continue the conversation. Shocked, I gave it to her. She wrote it on her hand as was the custom, smiled and turned to leave. I remember thinking at the time that it should have been sacrilege to mar such beautiful skin with ink. I also learned that I could respond to stimuli emotionally, without using my head. If this story had sound effects you would hear the sound of impending doom with that statement.

When the glow of instant celebrity had dimmed, I realized that I had a major problem. How was I going to convince my mother to let me use the phone? More importantly, we had not established a time for this telephone date. I was consumed for the rest of the day trying to figure out a plan. My only hope was that she would call before my mother got home at 5:30. But of course, that didn't happen. This importance of this telephone call was growing in momentum. It had developed a life of its own.

I decided that the only way to accomplish this was to be honest. To tell the truth and ask, plead my case, no beg to use the phone. My mother sat quietly as I explained the entire scenario, too quietly perhaps. This was approximately four months after the whole first kiss thing, so I suppose she knew this was coming. She asked one single question. Unfortunately, it was the one question I couldn't answer. "What time was I supposed to call her?" Without thinking, I blurted out; "she's going to call me". As a wry smile appeared on my mother's face, I proudly added "she asked me for my phone number". While trying to contain her growing amusement; she quipped "you don't have a phone number, I do". Then came the inevitable "What kind of parents let a kid use the phone, especially to call a boy speech?" What kind of a "fast" girl would even think of doing it? I tried to defend my girlfriend's honor and only succeeded in making me seem more desperate.

Finally, surprisingly my mother relented. Not only to let me use the telephone, but to keep it clear until Candace called. She put a stack of 45's on the stereo and went upstairs, leaving me to my vigil. It was 6:30.

Exactly one hour later the music stopped and she returned to call my brother and sister in from playing. "No, I wouldn't be eating dinner". I sat on the couch, my posture reflecting my slightly shaken confidence and knots of anticipation in my stomach.

She emerged from the kitchen and walked silently past the now obviously nervous figure lying on his side on the sofa. Another stack of 45's was placed on the stereo. Not even the sounds of Motown had any effect on my rapidly sinking mood.

My Timex taunted me. It was now after 8:00pm. My brother and sister finished their homework and chores and headed to bed asking if I was sick or something. I heard my mother's reply of "something". It was the last voice I remember other than the repeating refrain of Jerry Butler's "Only the Strong Survive" on the stereo. I was lying prone on the sofa. Face down on my stomach, arms at my side in the "closed" position. I awoke the next morning still guarding the phone.

The hardest part was still to come. I had to face Candace in second period French. I was extremely nervous about the meeting. What would I say? What would she say? The class came and went without incident or words. She did smile at me however, when we left lunch. My curiosity was getting the best of me, but I wasn't sure that I would get the chance to talk to her alone. My feelings were also bruised by her casual attitude.

I went to my detention after school; my punishment for being late that day. It allowed me time to focus for the first time that day. I did my homework and read ahead. Dejected, I left school for home and to my surprise ran right into Candace; who had just come from an extra-curricular meeting. As I approached her, I could still see the remnants of my phone number on her hand.

I cautiously brought up the telephone appointment. Looking surprised, she raised her hand to her face to look at the partially erased number. Then I made the mistake that reshaped my entire approach to women; that I still use today. I flatly asked her. Why hadn't she called as she said she would? She looked at me with an expressionless glare and said, "I guess I forgot to call". I stood there crushed as she turned and walked away. We never talked about the subject again. Nor did we ever talk on the phone, even though we remained friends through high school.

I had always been taught that the truth would set you free. That knowledge would lead to greater understanding and therefore the peace of closure and resolution. Nothing could be more incorrect. The "why" question almost always leads to pain; possibly anger, but definitely more questions. Questions lead to more doubt, denial, supposition and ultimately more questions. This creates an endless cycle of pain and soul searching that leads to depression and anything but closure. The lesson: accept the truth for what it is; focus on the facts without regard to the reason. It's far less painful and easier to put behind you.

# Chapter Four

## My Sister's Friends

Puberty; the disease we all contract. Some of us recover faster than others. Some of us never do. We all encounter wounds from the experience, but hopefully the lessons learned benefit us more than the scars disfigure. I'm sure you can recall some people that somehow slid through those years completely unscathed, but as you already know life has a way of leveling things. That's the main reason to go to class reunions, after all.

My voyage through puberty was at its minimum eventful and overwhelming at the maximum. This of course includes tremendous emotional highs and incredible gut wrenching lows. The significant fact is that the trip was memorable. I consider the puberty years to include junior high or middle school through college for most people. Why? Puberty is about exploration, discovery and recognition. Unfortunately, as everybody knows our minds are well behind our bodies and hormones. Consequently, we must take the entire journey before we learn all the lessons necessary to successfully enter adulthood.

The first step on my voyage involves my sister's friends. My sister and I are only sixteen months apart in age. That single fact evens the playing field. Her friends were just about the same mental age and at a similar stage of physicality and curiosity as I was. This was a mutually beneficial relationship. They could disguise their interest in me by simply saying that they had just come over to see my sister. I similarly could pretend that I didn't know that they were coming over. My sister was allowed to go places she ordinarily wouldn't be able to go. The added benefit to her was that some of her friends had older brothers, and of course there also were my male friends.

They say that a girl's first boyfriend is her Dad. That being the case; pubescent girls need guinea pigs on which to practice and hone their skills. This arrangement was perfect for this purpose. The main reason this worked was because I was an eager participant. I mean this was a "hands on lab" to learn everything I could about the opposite sex. They wanted to play all of the requisite "rites of passage games"; "spin the bottle", "strip poker", and "hide and go get". The latter being an urban adaptation of hide and go seek, which could only be played after dark. It was of no real consequence who was "it". The object of the game was to either be chased and groped or found in a dark secluded spot. Great fun either way!

Secondly, it was our first official opportunity to "date". You had the chance to practice the art of in-person conversation, etiquette, and social responsibility. We took the bus to the movies, shopping or bowling. We would have lunch and head home. We were usually in groups, but sometimes we would venture off on our own and meet later to continue the illusion of having been in the "safety of numbers all day". I developed a couple of serious crushes in the process. I guess that's where I developed the philosophy of urgency, when spending time with a woman. Everything that you needed to do or say had to be done within the small window of time allotted by curfews and such. The result of the urgency concept was an intensity and passion that is hard to maintain, but easy to remember. And that's what life's all about isn't it; making memories.

# Chapter Five

## Maiden Voyage

### Part One

It was a warm Saturday in early autumn. I had spent the day washing, waxing and vacuuming my mother's car in preparation for my first car date. I had received my driver's license just a month earlier. It had taken that long to convince my mother to loan me the car. I had endured endless lectures about how her car had only one purpose, to get her to work. What did she know? Everything was planned except that there was no way to control the music. Her car was equipped with a stock AM radio. I promised myself that my first car was not only going to have FM stereo, but an 8-track tape player as well. That's how you really set the mood!

Earlier that week, I had asked out a girl in my class. She was tall and thin, smart, but very shy. She always chose to remain silent unless called upon on class, even though she knew the answers. She was high yellow. In black vernacular, that meant she was light-skinned. She had a touch of acne and long bushy medium brown hair. I was drawn to her pleasant disposition and seemingly limitless patience and interest in other people's stories. She seemed pleased when I asked her to go to the movies with me. When she hugged me after she accepted, the shy girl showed me a totally new and unexpected dimension. There was passion in her eyes. She kissed for keeps.

Now as I finished the car and contemplated wardrobe, my main problem was how to bring up the subject of the drive-in theater. The movie we had agreed to see was playing at the Vogue theatre just two miles from her house. It was a good initial plan, but after that acceptance kiss, the drive-in seemed like a much better option.

My expectations for the evening diminished rapidly when I met her mother. She was a darling woman who acted more like her grandmother than her mom. She talked for at least fifteen minutes before I saw my date. It was obvious that she had doted on and protected her only child. She gave me instructions as though I was taking a Faberge egg out on display, rather than dating her daughter. Having raised a daughter myself, I now know it's pretty much the same thing. All of her fears were allayed however, because we were in the living room. The living room belonged to me. It was a natural gift. I was a Boy Scout. Thoughtful, smart, prepared for any question. I was simultaneously sincere, flirty and resourceful. The living room was where mothers were coquettish and reminisced, while fathers feared and loaded their guns.

I really began to doubt my wisdom when my date finally descended the stairs. She was dressed simply, casually and probably purposefully on the juvenile side by her mother. She wore shorts, a blouse and canvas shoes. Minimal jewelry and make-up adorned her face. Her hair was in a loose ponytail with half-assed bangs. Still, she was as cute as she could be. Her mother insisted that she wear her sweater. But her final mood killer was her best. She insisted that I kiss her good-bye on the cheek, just like her daughter did.

As I opened the passenger door of the car for my date I casually said "the movie we decided to see is playing at the Vogue theatre in twenty minutes". I got in and started the car and slowly pulled away from the house. She said nothing until we reached the stop sign at the corner. While waiting my turn to go, she slid over next to me and said "it also starts at the drive-in in a half an hour." "We can get something to eat on the way". I turned and my sly smile matched hers. I really miss bench seats.

The rest of the date was a typical teenage make-out session. The movies were good. I guess. You had to watch enough of it to be able answer questions, if necessary. I was happy with my arrival at second base on the first date. I even complimented her on how pretty her lace bra was. That was until she was comfortable enough to open her purse and show me the matching panties she wasn't wearing. "It was in case someone checked them," she said sadly. It was then that we noticed that it was eleven twenty-five; curfew was midnight in those days, and not negotiable. That single fact immediately killed the mood and changed any thoughts I may have had. We gathered ourselves quickly and started on the journey home. However, the genie was already out of the bottle. Fortunately, she shared my philosophy of intensity and adventure. So with some excellent coaching on her part, and some deft digital work on mine, I was able to steal third while driving. With the crowd cheering; metaphorically of course, she announced rather loudly her arrival at home, just as the car did the same. We agreed to go out again next week. Now before you judge me too harshly, we were both sixteen and happy. More importantly, the poignant part of the story is detailed in part two.

Maiden Voyage

Part Two

The year was 2001. It was September, a full twenty-eight years
after that first date. The occasion was our first book club meeting of the new session. We met from September thru April on the
third Saturday of the month. This was our fifth year enjoying great
food, friendship and discussion of the works of Black authors,
current events and male/female issues from an Afro-centric perspective. Our educational, income, age and social demographics
were diverse, so discussions were always interesting and lively.
The first meeting was traditionally new members' night. We always
had grab bag topics to make them feel comfortable and give them
a chance to contribute on their first visit. I was scheduled to start
the festivities by virtue of winning "Speaker of the Year" honors
for the third straight year. I was flattered by the presenting group
that stated "it is impossible to distinguish whether his speeches are
so rehearsed as to seem spontaneous or so elegantly spontaneous
that they appear rehearsed." I was a little late in arriving and didn't
have time to greet everyone, before sitting down with a plate of
food and having the grab-bag thrust in my face. As I reached into
the bag for the subject of my five-minute speech, I noticed my old
friend in the corner. She sat as shy and reserved as she had always
been in high school. We had shared quite a few phone calls over
the years, so I knew she was in the middle of her second bad marriage. Her first husband was the guy she dumped me for in high
school.

She had gained more than a few pounds over the years, but otherwise she looked pretty much the same. Her warm caring eyes and
natural smile had survived the hard times.

I opened the scrap of paper and read silently "First Date". I took
a deep breath, let it out slowly and began. "My first car date was
with a tall, light skinned, skinny girl that greeted me with the
soothing warmth of her large brown eyes". The group let out an

"Awwww". "I later found out that the warmth was fueled by a blast furnace of passion that she had secretly hidden within". Loud "knowing" laughter echoed from the group. I continued. "She wore small pink lump crystal earrings and a matching ring. Green culottes and a pageboy collared, white sleeveless blouse with pink and green flowers on it. Her mother made her wear a pink cable knit sweater, even though it was too warm to need it". The crowd was silenced and enthralled by the detail of my remembrance of the occasion. "Her shoes were khaki canvas slip-ons with raffia trim around the soles." "She smelled of Jergens lotion and baby powder." "Her hair started the date in a loose ponytail and bangs, that she quickly brushed into the long flowing mane that I was accustomed to seeing." "I don't mean to embarrass her but she had on a blue lace"… suddenly the silence was broken by sobbing from the corner. Everyone's attention focused on the quiet new member that had been invited by a mutual friend. She whined through the tears "he's talking about me". She continued "I can't believe he remembered a date with me after all these years" I stood and walked toward her. She met me halfway with a hug and said, "thank you". I released her when she stopped crying as the group applauded. When she took her seat she said, "If I didn't come home tonight, my husband wouldn't know what to tell the police I was wearing today." The tension eased as everyone laughed. Then a man said, "I want to hear more about the blue lace and how he knew", unleashing more laughter from the group. I thought to myself, I didn't even get to the pink lip-gloss that matched her fingernail polish.

# Chapter Six

## First Dates

## Analysis

In my opinion, all dates should be that memorable. Impossible you say! Well, I believe that if you choose your partners carefully and discriminately. Then give your all to make the date fun and interesting, it's not that difficult. Dating is almost a lost art. It doesn't surprise me that conversation is also in similar distress. Sure, we have a plethora of communication devices, but we still actually connect with people less than we used to. Take the time to notice people when you're out. You'll find couples having dinner; look closer and you'll see that they aren't even talking to each other. He may be watching the game on TV; she could be talking to someone on the phone. These aren't always "old married couples" either.

# Chapter Seven

## High School Sweetheart

## Missed Opportunity?

Never has there been a more misunderstood young lady than my high school sweetheart. When the term sweetheart was invented, I'm certain that they used her as the model. She was as kind, patient, compassionate, dedicated and loving as the average three people could be. She accomplished this amazing feat seemingly with minimal effort. It just came naturally. Always smiling; she contributed a major share of the care her younger sisters needed, and they adored her. In fact, everyone did. She belonged to a close knit sorority of friends that was named after a delicious dessert. Their bond was impenetrable. They were fiercely loyal and supportive. These were the qualities that she possessed singularly. She graduated co-valedictorian, National Honor Society, Human Relations and the Majorettes; which is where I met her as a band member.

A quiet classmate; she was almost invisible. She was well dressed but not a slave to fashion. She sat with her legs crossed demurely at the ankles, wearing outdated cat-eyed glasses to see the board. I had several classes with her and we shared a few club memberships. Taking the chance to ask her out on a date was the best risk I ever took.

Our first date was normal enough, but I quickly learned that there was a certain duality to her personality. She was such a wonderful person. So much so, that I hesitate to say anything that would place any doubt on the character or opinion of this special person. But knowing her, she would want me to tell the truth. To be honest, she really never committed a major faux pas. The fact is, it was just practically impossible to live up to her image. In retrospect, trying to do so may have been a significant part of her struggles.

She loved to have fun; craved excitement and loved to laugh. She also enjoyed taking chances, nothing really serious; certainly no more than we all did, it just didn't fit her stereotype. I mean she knew more make out spots than I did. Being with her was exhilarating.

Early in our relationship she called me; asking me to pick her up so we could "make out". Unable to resist an invitation like that, I drove to her house. As I exited the car, I heard rustling in the bushes and soon she came running from the side of the house waving me back to the car. We made out like wildcats that night; partly I'm certain due to the excitement of her sneaking out of the house.

We were inseparable; well outside of classes, club meetings, and homework, work and band performances. She just added the responsibility of girlfriend to everything else. And like everything else, she took it seriously and excelled. We had the same philosophy about our time together: intensity.

She defended me fiercely. Once she did a minor paper for me. We had the same class at different times during the day. She was furious when I told her that I had received a C+ on the paper. I was satisfied. Then she showed me the almost exact same paper that she had submitted; it had received an A. She was after all, an A student. She confronted the teacher; risking her reputation, against my advice. She hated injustice.

Our energy and chemistry was obvious to all of our classmates. We were a couple that everyone assumed would get married. We used that enthusiasm as fuel for our candidacy for Homecoming King and Queen. We ran a great campaign in a very large high school. We were the underdogs as we ran against star athletes, cheerleaders and beauty queens. In our high school; the campaign was a true popularity contest, with posters, slogans, speeches and rallies. We finished a very respectable third, but most importantly the campaign brought us closer together. Everything was perfect until the Christmas break.

This was our second Christmas break together and I was hoping that it wouldn't be like the first. I worked a lot of overtime and for whatever reason, she was rarely available. It was tough on the relationship. We argued for the first and only time. This year had to be different. There was a very important party that I wanted to take her to between Christmas and New Years Eve. The plans were made and everything was set. I was getting dressed when I received a tearful phone call; it seemed that she couldn't make it. She wouldn't elaborate.

Deflated, dejected and frankly angry, I went to the party anyway. I wasn't myself. My thoughts were split between her and what was wrong with me. My pain must have been obvious to everyone; that and the fact that we were never seen apart. One of my best friends that had always been there for me came up to me and said "that we should go outside and talk". She was also in my girlfriend's sorority. She was not one to beat around the bush, so as soon as we got outside on the unusually warm night, she hit me between the eyes with the news. She looked directly in my eyes and said; "you know she has a boyfriend that's in college". "I couldn't stand to see you suffer anymore". I wanted to be deaf. I wanted to go back in time and prevent her from saying that. But it was too late.

I stood in the driveway drowning, overwhelmed by the flood of emotions and questions running through my mind, causing the churning in my stomach. I couldn't breathe or move. I must have stood there for a half an hour in a trance. I hated her. I hated myself for hating her. I left the party and went home and to bed. My body parts were acting independently; mind racing, my heart torn to shreds, stomach in knots. Sleep was impossible. Ultimately, by morning I just wanted to see her. I wanted to hear her explain the inexplicable. There was no reason for her friend to lie about it. She was good friends with both of us.

It was Tuesday morning before I received a phone call from her. A small voice on the other end of the line said simply, "Please come and see me. I need to talk to you". I told her flatly, that I had to work in the afternoon, but I would come by around six.

My attempts at concentration were futile that afternoon. I thought I had covered all of her possible answers by the time I had left work. I drove to her house feeling confident that I was ready for her explanation, but I had no idea how I would react to seeing her. I walked to her door like a man heading to the electric chair. The only sound I heard was my heart beating in my chest, louder and louder as approached her front door. The door opened slowly while she hid behind it. I entered the dark living room and waited for my eyes to adjust. She appeared out of the shadows wearing a knee length flannel gown. She wasn't trying to seduce me. She looked awful. Her hair was mussed. Her normal make-up was replaced with red eyes surrounded by puffy blue-black circles. The rest of her face was colorless; her lips were chapped. She looked as though she had neither slept nor showered in days.

My broken heart melted and I reached out for her. She burst into tears as she ran toward me. I held her as she shook and tried to talk. She was crying "real" tears. By "real" I mean these tears weren't for her. She was sorry and embarrassed by what she had done to me. She apologized profusely and admitted her guilt. Her guilt was so strong that she confessed that she was the one who had told her friend to tell me. Her embrace was therapeutic. She didn't look at me. She just kept adjusting her grip as though she was trying to absorb the pain from my body. It was working. We lay together on the sofa for hours, as she tearfully explained her dilemma between requests for me to hold her tighter. "She wanted to remember this moment forever," she said. She also did any and everything she could to make sure I did too.

The news of our break-up spread like wildfire at school after the holidays. The facts of the case remained a secret, but the fallout was wide spread. The prom was coming up and there were two new prize contenders on the market. The reality was that there was only one new person on the market. My ex-girlfriend had chosen her college boyfriend over me. I was the odd man out.

We ran into each other occasionally, she always smiled warmly when we met, but I never really recovered. We graduated and she went off to college without incident. I didn't realize it at the time, but I had discovered a trait in her that would ultimately be her downfall.

We didn't see each other again until two years later; in traffic. She beckoned me to follow her home. Once there she hugged me as though nothing had ever happened. The warmth in her eyes and smile took me back, but things were different now. We talked about how tough college had been; what our plans were; when she suddenly burst into "real" tears. She asked me to lay with her for old-time's sake. Her voice quivered, as she recounted the painful story of rejection and betrayal administered by her former college boyfriend. She then apologized to me again, saying it was only after her gut wrenching experience, that she truly knew what I had gone through. She felt herself a fool in retrospect considering the chances she had taken, places she had gone and sacrifices made to keep that relationship. It was then, that I realized that her traits were becoming more pronounced. She vowed to be there for me for "anything" I needed. She took me into her one final time. It was a deep, warm, healing embrace that left no doubt about the sincerity of her pledge. She went back to school in the fall. I never saw her again.

I heard some out of character remarks about her, and the person she was with at a Holiday function, but I didn't think too much about it. Many of my friends that had gone away to school were "different" than they used to be. It was expected. I didn't attend any of the holiday gatherings; so any information that I received was gossip anyway. Still, if the gossip were true it would be disturbing.

The following summer was an eventful one. Among other things, I got married. Most of my friends had returned to town after graduating from college. It was a time of great promise, hope and camaraderie. There was a picnic and card party being planned to reacquaint everyone. We were all looking forward to it. We couldn't imagine at the time that the joyous event we were planning would be supplanted by a funeral. It was a funeral that would shake us all to the bedrock of our beliefs and force us to confront our own fragile existence.

My high school sweetheart had been found dead; killed by a single gunshot to the head, apparently while arguing with the disturbing person she had been linked to by rumors I didn't want to believe.

It was said that they argued about marriage. If that was true; then her trait of throwing away happiness to seek out places that she did not fit had finally caught up with her. The only thing I knew for sure was that it was a terrible tragedy and I missed her. The whole world was a darker place without her smile. Many of her classmates acted as pallbearers in the funeral service; silently and seamlessly rotating in and out. I was the only one who carried her casket the entire way. I just couldn't let go. A fact that was not lost on my new wife; I might add. My sister who knows me better than anyone on earth says that, "the only times she ever saw me truly happy was when I was with her". She just may be right.

## Just One Kiss from You

While gazing into your mile-deep eyes, I am humbled by your
grace.
I marvel at the beautiful portrait, simply called your face.
The musical sound of your precious voice brings joy of a special kind.
While a soothing breeze from your delicate lashes floats gently
across my mind.
These many visions you portray that are so uniquely you, are what
cause my heart to fly.
To a special place where passion thrives and dreams soar; while
sadness quickly dies.
I'm transported there emotionally, in a way no other force can do.
All these things are possible, with just one kiss from you.
I survey the contours of your nose, visually sample a silken cheek.
The feel of your tender, loving arms around me makes my legs go weak.
Supported by the curve of her hips; held up by her hair.
Wrapped snugly in love's web; my lungs devoid of air.
Summoned by the rhythm of your hypnotic breathing.
Hearts all a flutter now, not just merely beating.
I stand there frail and motionless; paralyzed by your charm.
But your gentle smile and warm embrace revives my stricken arms.
Admiring the subtle curvature of your neck;
I gain the courage to take a chance, to risk just one peck.
Drawn in by your magnetic breath, past where your porcelain
pearls are strung.
First, my soul is caressed by the delicacy of your lips.
Then I am pulled in deeper, and nourished by your tongue.
At that moment, I realize just how special life and love can be.
In an instant; an everlasting, magic bond is forged between thee and me.
My mind shut down; eyes closed tight, your beauty still in view.
Ecstasy and bliss miraculously found, with just one kiss from you.

James Robert Russell

## Chapter Nine

### Encounters with Older Women

The next stage of my social development came abruptly on the heels of my exposure to my sister's friends. The time I spent as the "chew toy" of older girls and women was probably the most beneficial to my development of all. In the beginning, at about fifteen I suddenly became attractive to them and I'm not sure why exactly; it could have been my physical stature as I had just experienced a growth spurt. It may have been my new found confidence having dealt with my sister's friends. Or it may have been the fact that I was financially well off for my age. I had a large and very profitable paper route plus two jobs. Possessing a great wardrobe, money in the bank, and a good head on my shoulders I had a bright future. However, I'd like to believe that at least some of it was due to the fact that I was just a nice guy. I am confident that I did surprise some of them with my maturity and exposure. But I harbor no illusions that I was in control of the situations.

In my teenage years, the girls that I attracted were two to seven years my senior. This took a totally different mindset than I was used to when it came to interpreting their actions and words. Their "teasing" wasn't. It was actually more of a challenge to me to impress them. Their words were often harsher than their younger counterparts, but at the same time they also knew when to shut-up and go with the flow. When dating younger girls you left the house with a lot of hopes. Those hopes became expectations with the older ones. I was able to get them into clubs that served alcohol because of my size and savvy. I didn't discriminate; I dated girls from every ethnicity, learning more about women as I went. This did even more to broaden my appeal. Honestly, I was having a ball.

To be perfectly clear, I was actually very selective about the women I dated. I could afford to be. Each encounter not only provided great fun, valuable experience, and wonderful memories, but it also narrowed my sights. By dating increasingly special and interesting women my outlook became jaded. This made it increasingly difficult to date women my own age. They just didn't measure up. In fact, I only seriously dated two; my high school sweetheart and the woman I fell head over heels in love with and eventually married.

I would also like to state for the record, that if it seems that I was calloused and uncaring in these relationships, exactly the opposite is true. The relationships ended when my partners wanted them to. Not once did I break up with any of them; additionally all of the break-ups were amicable. Amazingly, to this day I can still remember the first and last names of over ninety-five percent of the women I dated. With particular emphasis on the word dated. Yes, there was passion and romance in all of the relationships, but actual intercourse in very few. Looking back on those times, it is amazing that some of the best relationships were never "consummated". As we all know; sex can often times complicate and ultimately ruin a perfectly good relationship.

It is also important for me to note that I never cheated on either my wife or my high school sweetheart. Those relationships were in a separate category. I value and hold the sanctity of marriage in high esteem. However, that being said; when I was told that the marriage was over; having done everything that I could to save it, I moved on. A trait that I wish I could have maintained later in life. More on that issue later.

When I was available in my twenties due to marital discourse my admirers were seven to ten years older than I. They had married when they were young and probably wanted to recapture that "lost time". I had entered the business world by this time and was rising fairly rapidly, due mostly to confidence, intelligence and "intangible skills" rather than formal education. These skill sets along with my genuine compassion are what probably won over fair ladies. Again, I am not saying that I was in control of these situations. Besides; the notion of control is overrated. I just wanted everything they had to give, plus a little that they didn't know they had. I gave them the same in return. These dear creatures had been bruised emotionally. I simply bandaged their wounds and healed them with kindness. If I had a gift; it was the ability to see what they could be, if only they had support and believed in themselves.

In turn, they showered me with cascades of pent-up affection for setting them free. Unfortunately, like an injured bird they flew away as soon as they were healed. I'd like to think that they left me feeling a little better about themselves than when I met them; I know I was richer for having known them.

As time wore on however; I realized that despite the feeling of warmth and accomplishment, the effort and emotion expended was taking its toll on me. I couldn't help being the person that I was; but the pain of repeatedly losing women was creating an increasingly larger hole in my heart that was endangering my very existence. Something had to be done.

The relationships have produced some poignant moments however. I was driving westbound on I-76 returning from a weeklong business trip. It was a great spring day; traffic was light, so I was tooling along at about 70 mph. I was taking advantage of the windshield time; enjoying the scenery. A Buick from Virginia passed me at about 80 mph. I noticed the woman in the passenger seat and mused to myself, she certainly looks a lot like Maureen.

My mind took me back to the first time I saw Maureen. She was of medium build and tall, about five foot nine. Possessing ginger-brown streaked hair in a modified page boy cut that framed large transparent light brown eyes. Her nose wrinkled when she laughed; rearranging the freckles that dotted her cheeks and nose. Ample, but not full lips guarded a professionally enhanced smile.

Long honey brown legs dangled from cuffed linen shorts. She walked toward me wearing thick, cabled bobby socks and girls tennis shoes. Upon reaching me she extended a neatly manicured, feminine hand saying, "You're just as my cousin described". She coyly looked downward while slowly swiveling on her heels with one knee bent. Her hand lingered in mine, as I pondered how much trouble I was in. As I stood in her baby lotion scent cloud, I deducted that she was far more polished than her seventeen years would suggest. I also felt suddenly younger than my already young fourteen and one-half years. I had grown up in a predominately black neighborhood; from her phraseology I determined that she hadn't.

Our first date consisted of one hour of getting to know you conversation, and two hours of I'm glad to know you kissing. Being slightly insecure, I asked her the following day to critique my performance. As she smiled and turned to walk away looking over her shoulder, she called back to me "a solid C plus". She continued, winking, "so we have a lot of practicing to do".

The Buick was more than a half a mile ahead, but I was catching up quickly. As I caught them, they signaled and moved to the fast lane. Pulling even with them, I recognized her immediately. Smiling, she waved me to the side of the road. Alternatively, I pointed to a Rest Area Ahead sign. It seemed like the longest mile I had ever driven. I parked in the rest area parking lot, took a deep breath and exited the vehicle. I watched two figures leave the Buick. An unidentified man accompanied her. She had gained a couple of "happy pounds", but other than that she looked virtually the same. I had taken two steps toward her when she began to run toward me. I quickly glanced toward the man for non-verbal clues. No reaction. She ran right through my extended arms, her body hitting me like a tsunami. Grabbing my face in both hands, she kissed me just as she had almost eighteen years earlier.

She then stretched out her arms to look at me. Her smile was electric, her eyes magnetic and in a warm alto voice she excitedly uttered "You look great!" Pulling me close again, she kissed me once more. This time gently and lingering. When she pulled away slowly; allowing me to breathe, I said dreamily, "It's good to see you." "You're lovelier now than you were then." She took my hand and started toward the man, who was still waiting patiently by the car. "You must meet my husband," she said cheerfully. Before I had a chance to panic, she called out "Honey, this is James." "He is the man that led me to you". We shook hands, his name was Walter. Maureen explained "that she knew that our summer romance would have never survived the distance, and test of time that high school and college would have imposed, but in me she had found the traits that she wanted in a husband."

With the situation now disarmed, she took each of our hands and led us to a picnic table where we sat for nearly an hour talking about our children. But I sensed or maybe just hoped, that we both were secretly reminiscing about the magical summer we spent together. I received my answer as we parted. She looked back over her shoulder, just the way she had done that day and winked saying, "A plus, you've been practicing".

# Oasis

Every man; if he is blessed, has a shelter from the storm.

The type of place that has faith for doors, and love to keep him warm.

Inside these walls, is protection from the pelting of life's grief.

Elevated confidence and boosted strength, fueled by her belief.

Instinctively, she senses his need for her gift.

Flashing her smile and reaching out; she gives her man a lift.

Kind words and special deeds; attending to his need.

Giving all she has; nothing held back, no expectations or greed.

His wounds all healed; ego mended, she sends him back to war.

His newly found courage and added strength, makes his spirits soar.

He returns to her with bounty, the rewards of his toils.

Both sustenance and tribute; to the victor goes the spoils.

She is his oasis, harbor in rough seas.

The only place he can drop his guard, and truly just be he.


James Russell

My mid to late twenties were wrought with marital discourse; broken promises, disillusion, bitter arguments and separations. My only sanity was my relationship with my children and my work. This story is about a chance encounter that sometimes haunts me to this day.

Anxious to get home to my children for my scheduled weekend visitation, I sped through the north woods to get to Grand Rapids, MI for my 3:30 flight. The airport was not large, nor was the city and it was prior to their "rush hour". I knew a couple of short cuts; after all I caught this flight every Friday to Cleveland; the last of the day. These were simpler times, pre 911. Cash payments were accepted at the last minute; there was minimal security, and no luggage fees. You could run right to the gate. But on this Friday, everything would go wrong and I missed the flight. "No flights to Cleveland or anywhere else in Ohio" was what the pleasant voice told me. Sensing my disappointment, she began the steps that sent me on a trip to serendipity.

## Chapter Eleven

### Coco

The reservationist had cleverly booked me on a roundabout passage destined for Cleveland. It was of course the last thing I needed on a Friday, after a long week on the road. But to get back home to my kids, I would have flown halfway around the world. I would come close to it. My itinerary was set. From Grand Rapids I flew to Detroit (I could have taken a direct flight from there, but that would have meant a seven-hour layover) from there to Minneapolis and finally to Cleveland. Seasoned business travelers understand the next part. This convoluted route was actually cheaper that my original plans, but I digress.

The first leg of the flight was uneventful. It was a short flight, no beverage service. There was plenty of time to change airlines and terminals in Detroit, where I boarded a "direct flight" to Minneapolis. For the uninitiated, this means trying to find a suitable seat on an already crowded plane. I reluctantly select a dreaded middle seat and squeeze to the seated position. Exhausted, I did something that I had never done and have not done since. The simple act of reclining my seat changed my entire outlook on life. I leaned back unsuccessfully, trying to find a comfortable position for my not built for coach class frame. My first glance into the row behind me revealed a pair of small, delicate hands holding a book. My initial impression of the evenly colored hands was mannequin-like perfection.

She held the book close, as if she were farsighted; hiding her face. The hands moved to turn a page. I nervously returned the seat back to its upright position. I sat there, stuck between inquisitive and afraid. After a few tortured moments, I reclined the seat again to get another peek at her.

As soon as I looked in her direction, she lowered the book to her lap and looked directly at me. Caught, I panicked and sat up straight in my seat, this time without using the seat as an aid. My heart was racing, partly from being caught, but mostly from what my quick glance had discovered. She had a roundish face which contained beautifully, a mouth overstocked with dazzlingly white teeth that when combined with ample pouting lips made for a devilishly inviting smile. The perfectly sized and subtly chiseled nose, expertly placed between graceful cheek bones were almost rendered unmentionable by the over whelming feature on her classically lovely face. Her unusually large brown eyes were framed by perfectly tailored brows, which were partially concealed by equally manicured bangs. Her magnificent orbs had infra-red warmth that beckoned your full attention. Having regained my composure, I leaned back in my already reclined seat. I turned to look in her direction, where she was patiently waiting for me. The glow from her eyes relaxed me as she spoke. Time seemed to slow down. "Coco" she said "My name is Coco." Emphasis on the first hard "C" then elongated (o) s that resonated in my head. The words floated by me in a mesmerizing French accent. I replied mechanically, "My name is Jim." She repeated "Jim." It sounded different coming from her mouth. She smiled warmly, seemingly amused and returned to her book. I sat up with my ego bruised and said nothing for the remainder of the flight.

That was not to say that I didn't think about our brief encounter. Being an accountant, I analyzed every facet of our initial meeting and concluded that it was an absolute failure. A brief announcement from the cockpit put the icing on the cake. We were to be the last flight in or out of the airport for an undetermined amount of time, due to fog. My hopes of having an opportunity to speak to her again, and redeem myself were dashed upon landing by the impatient urging of the passenger in the window seat. He was in a hurry to go nowhere. She was blocked by a woman with a small child, who was in no hurry at all. Silently accepting defeat, I deplaned.

I wandered through the concourse ignoring all the faces of despair. Zombies, all given the sentence of "departure time unknown" for the crime of airline travel. Through the crowd, I noticed an oasis in the form of an ice cream kiosk. I headed directly toward it. I noticed for the first time the dense, cotton candy-like mist outside. It was thicker than the mood inside the terminal. We were going to be here a long time. When it was finally my turn to order, I said in a surprisingly upbeat voice, "two dips of butter pecan in a cup." Just then someone grasped my arm from behind, as I reached for my pocket. A voice said "make that two please, but I'd like mine on a sugar cone." We turned simultaneously to face each other for the first time, and in unison said "it's the only flavor of ice cream I eat." She deftly paid the clerk and retrieved her treat with one hand, as the other never left my arm. She led me away from the stand and said "Jim, I had hoped that I would see you again, Jim." She smiled as she made reference to our awkward initial encounter. As we walked toward a row of chairs, I noticed that she was not tall, but like her face her body was in perfect proportion. Her movements though subtle and feminine; were purposeful and confident. Reaching the row of chairs we sat, she with a flourish as she spun, sat and crossed her legs in one motion, all without taking her hand from my arm or my face from her gaze.

We talked about life, love, politics and economics. Her eyes were backlit when she was excited, exhibiting a kaleidoscope of brown

hues from amber to sienna. They would fill with water as she recounted stories of poverty in countries she had visited. Amazingly,
however she never shed a tear. The conversation was spirited.
We shared ideas; disagreed on concepts. We finished each other's
sentences, without stepping on private thoughts. She was intelligent and funny, insightful and kind. She was sexy without intend-
ing to be, evidenced by how she ate her ice cream. She blinked
often, slowly, rhythmically with lashes that brought to mind the
giant feathers of attendants fanning their queen. I don't know if the
purpose was to fan my passion or to cool hers, as she seemingly,
effortlessly broke the rhythm with a seductive slow wink when she
agreed with me. But it worked for me.

Her voice was a symphony, sometimes as light and perky as a
piccolo, at other times the soulful moan of the cello seemed to fit.
Her words were carried on the melody of her accent. She was four
years younger than I, but her experiences belied that difference.
She had been raised and educated in Europe, and was currently
pursuing a Master's degree at a college outside of Seattle, the final
destination of her trip. It was as if her parents knew exactly how
she would turn out at birth. She was named brilliantly. Her flawless
skin was the color of rich hot chocolate lightened with a dollop of
whipped cream. Her long thick hair featured soft curls like the (c) s
in her name. She was warm and soothing; sweet, but complex and
rich in an attainable way. She was beautiful in everything she did
and was. The amazing fact was that she seemed totally unaware of
it.

Our ice cream now finished, she turned to face me. She took hold
of my wrists with my hands palms down in both of her smallish
hands; she ran then them up my forearms until she reached the
elbow. Then with me still locked in her amber, magnetic gaze she
returned her hands slowly to my wrists, gently pushing my hands
down to her now exposed thighs, just above the knee. I will never
forget the sound she made when first I touched, then squeezed her
silken limbs. She guided my hands slowly higher as she inched
forward, toward a first kiss. The exhilarating drama was happening
in super slow-motion. We were completely oblivious to the rest of
the world. My fingers were slithering under the hem of her skirt,
as her knees began to part. Our lips were almost touching. I was

an instant from tasting her when we were jolted back to reality by a loud PA announcement that the airport had reopened. Instantly, the mood was broken and the magnetic lamps in her eyes switched off. She leaned back pushing her hips forward to stretch her legs in front of her. Her movement forced my hands completely under her skirt and caused her to make that heavenly sound again. It was a primal cooing sound that seemed to emanate from her soul. If that type of sound could have a language, it would definitely be French.

My flight to Cleveland was announced over the PA system. She suddenly leaned forward and cupped my face in both hands and in classic film noir fashion said "I will go wherever you go" in her heaviest accent yet. For the first time, she seemed not to be in control. Her breathing was quicker, heavier, her top lip quivering. The lights in her eyes brightened and pulsated, as if they were milk chocolate searchlights beckoning me to her shore. However, the look on my face must have delivered the message that my lips had the sense not to utter.

Deflated she initially leaned back, then stood still holding my wrists forcing me to stand as well. I stood there like a noble suit of armor, saying not a word. I turned to leave as the voice on the PA announced the final boarding call for my flight. She took the first step with me, as I looked at her longingly, incredulously. Our second step was halted by a different voice over the PA, calling all passengers heading to Seattle for the final time. The first announcement must have been ignored while we were in our "trance." She stepped closer gently putting her head in my chest, while looking straight ahead. I noticed the tropical smell of her hair for the first time. "You could spend a lifetime with her and discover something new every day." I chuckled silently to myself. She said "Jim, remember me forever Jim." "Coco." The delivery of the words, especially her name was unforgettable, her voice was urgent. When she looked up at me for the final time, I noticed she had shed a single tear. Without waiting for an answer, she turned and scurried away. I watched as she reached the end of the concourse. She turned and looked back, seemingly to give me one final chance to change my mind.

I could still see and feel the warmth of her tear filled eyes beckoning to me. I stood motionless and watched my soul mate take a journey to the isle of what could have been, in the sea of lost opportunities. Whisked away by what I could have or should have said.

As my plane took off for home it was my turn to shed a single tear, as I quietly uttered her name. "Coco".

## The Meaning of Sweetest Day

To recognize not just the sweet, but the Sweetest, the best.

Not just the one you love, the one you love more than the rest.

You give them your passion, absorb their pain.

You're there for them, even when no one else remains.

You give more than you can, devotion, energy, infinite trust.

Anything less for love wouldn't be just.

Every moment apart a dull aching pain.

Waking thoughts ask, "When will I see her again?"

Arms long to hold her; to feel her touch.

A single day to remind her that you love her so much.


Lovingly,


Jim

# Cayenne

Cherry red powder; fiery hot taste.

Spicy and vibrant personality, she has energy to waste.

Sometimes quick to anger, always ready to cuss.

If you think that's all she's about then you've missed the bus.

Just beneath the peel she's tender, and so very sweet.

The warmest, kindest woman, you're likely ever to meet.

She endures heartache and abuse of the very worst kind,

While her long neglected essence of love withers on the wine.

The tragedy of this story is; that it really need not be.

The only thing she needs to thrive is an understanding he.

Someone to cultivate her roots; give shelter from the sun.

A gardener to nourish and support; so she can have some fun.

If that someone comes along, and actually helps her to grow.

Then he'll find himself in a better place than he could hope to know.

For when he showers her with the tenderness that lets her passion loose.

He'll find that the real flavor of cayenne is not the powder, but the juice.

James Robert Russell

The Delicacy Called Woman

The heat of the Fire,

The look in her Eyes,

The sweetness of Wine,

The sound of her Voice,

The feel of her Skin,

The numbing tingle of Ice,

The freshness of the first spring Breeze,

The grace of her Movement,

She creases my Memory,

Makes me Smile,

She takes me on a Journey,

How she makes me Feel!

The glow of her Smile,

The light of the Stars,

The gentle pounding of her Heart,

The beat of the Drum,

The whisper of Victoria's Secret,

The rustle of Leaves,

The rhythmic tapping of her high Heels,

The patter of Rain,

She lights my Path,

Makes me Dream,

She lightens my Load,

Takes away the Pain.

James Russell

# Chapter Fifteen

## Nikki

It was December in the early eighties. The holiday season, though one of my personal favorites was again proving to be emotionally challenging. I was separated from my family, no more accurately from my ex-wife. This was my second of three separations and the longest. It was a Saturday night and I was preparing to go to the company holiday party. Being separated put me in the middle of that dark vacuum called loneliness. Seasonal outings like this one, only magnified that feeling. Socially, I could have skipped this party, but in terms of my career; my attendance was mandatory.

The party was well attended. Everyone brought someone it seemed, except me. I mingled and moved constantly to avoid being a drag on anyone's time. I didn't want to be the dreaded third wheel. I was managing fairly well until I was cornered by the company president; who was gaudily attired, complete with a lighted and musical holiday tie. He persuaded me with a rather heavy hand that it was in my best interest to join the group he was assembling to do the Bunny Hop. After ten minutes of exhausting embarrassment, I was able to slip away to a quiet corner to metaphorically lick my wounded ego.

It was there that I encountered my buddy Mike. Mike was the spiritual leader of our rat pack. The rest of us weren't exactly chopped liver, but he was the real ladies man. Think Tom Selleck with reddish-brown hair in a shirt and tie. I had started a conversation with him, filling him in on what he had missed. I was glad to see him, and shocked to find him alone. I was just about to comment on that rare phenomenon, when the door to the ladies room opened and two women emerged and strode toward Mike. That's more like it, I thought to myself.

Mike introduced the ladies as they approached. The first was named Michelle; she was a tall, thin, fair skinned brunette. She was pleasant and energetic. She eventually became Mike's wife. The other woman was of average height with thick auburn hair. She had freckles, pouty lips and a cute little upturned nose. She was classically and expensively dressed. Her only show of flashiness was the three rhinestones on her hose, just above the ankles. I decided to eat dinner with this group, and it was an excellent choice. They were all excellent conversationalists, and for the first time that evening, I felt like I belonged. Nikki had a quiet confidence and a raspy voice that contrasted with her overall image of femininity.

Mike and Michelle were obviously in love. It was odd to see him act this way with a woman. They eventually left the table to mingle, leaving me alone with Nikki. We continued our conversation and it was going well, but it was still a very strange situation. Neither of us had anywhere else to go. But we weren't really together either. Her warm brown eyes smiled as much as her mouth as she talked. I didn't think much of it, other than she was trying to make the best of an awkward evening. I offered to get her a drink, both to be a gentleman and to clear my head. I was enjoying her company more than I probably should. I watched her from the bar and noticed just how poised and mature she was, belying her mere twenty-four years of experience. I placed her drink on the table while I was still standing. She looked up and said, "You certainly show a girl a nice time". She demurely looked down, revealing the thickest pair of eyelashes I had ever seen. Without looking up she said, "Maybe we could have a dance?" "That's a great idea," the voice said from behind me. Mike had returned to the table with Michelle. Michelle nudged her college friend and said smiling, "you two seemed to have gotten on without us".

Meanwhile, I was panic stricken. I was a pretty decent at ballroom dance at one time. It was before reconstructive knee surgery on both legs that robbed me of both mobility and confidence. Normally, a dance was just a dance. However, this was a different situation. This was a work function, and I felt as though I was on display. Then there was also the whole separation thing. To top it off, this was a woman that I had never even walked across the room with, let alone held. Nikki didn't wait for an answer. She stood, took my hand and strode toward the dance floor. The warmth and softness of her smallish hand calmed my nerves a bit, but I could still feel every eye in the room on us. As we made our way to the center of the floor the DJ played "Broken Wings" by Mister, Mister. Nikki turned and said, "I love this song". Well we had that it common, I thought. We started the dance a respectable distance apart. It was similar to a dance class stance. The music had transformed her. The first thing that I noticed was her posture. It was perfect. Her footwork was fluid and feminine, but precise. Her eyes were doe like, while flashing intensity. She adapted beautifully to my initial clumsiness, and by the chorus she had closed the distance between us and moved into me.

"Hold me tighter" she said almost urgently, as she turned her head with a flourish. Her movements were both graceful and intuitive. We danced as though we had rehearsed this routine for weeks. Everyone else had obviously noticed as well. As our movements grew larger, the other dancers relented and moved aside to watch us. The scene was reminiscent of a Hollywood musical, planned spontaneity; professionally executed. Passion was written all over her face, but I didn't think it was for me necessarily. She just loved to dance.

In preparation for a final maneuver, I pushed her away for a lengthy spin. I along with the entire room marveled at her grace. I spun inside of her and pulled her rapidly toward me. Our bodies met with arched backs and opposing arms above our heads. I locked her other arm behind her. As her hips crashed into mine, she uttered a raspy little whimper that stunned me. We began to sway together with the music, her eyes fixed on me. I asked her if she was hurt. Nikki looked down, offering me another view of those incredible lashes, and with those pouting lips she admitted demurely, whispering, "I had an orgasm". As the song ended and applause began, she politely curtsied, looked at me one last time and scurried off the dance floor. I didn't see her again that evening, or ever again.

I stood there embarrassed, undeserving of the applause, suddenly feeling terribly alone and shorter somehow. I walked off the dance floor being particularly careful not to trip or fall. As I finished my dessert, I replayed the magical moment in my head. Her grace had raised my mediocre ability to a level that I have not since approached. One dance temporarily erased my problems and gave me peace. I still miss that feeling.

My experience with Nikki is an excellent example of the types of brushes with greatness that I've encountered with women. Although some of the relationships lasted a fair amount of time; they all ended suddenly, unexpectedly and usually with great emotional pain.

## Love's Light

Sudden, subtle heat that dries the heaven's tears

Expanding, faint light that removes midnight's fears

Clouds illuminated in majesty, sky streaked in fiery glory

A kaleidoscope of color spotlights another day's story

The birth of a new day, a chance to redeem

A fresh opportunity to fulfill a long held dream

As the light and heat rises, so do thoughts of hope

Nurturing inside you the strength to endure, and patience to cope

Light chases away the shadows; warmth replaces cold

The miraculous sight actually returns youth to the old

The dawn of the day on which we've come to depend

Symbolizes a new day's beginning, not yesterday's end

Yet another chance to mend fences, heal wounds, create memories that last

Instead most remain mired, clinging to their soul robbing past


James R. Russell

Chapter Seventeen

Travel Companions

Grace

The best part about getting older is being able to look back on the great times, experiences and sights you've seen. Well after thirty years of business travel most of my best moments can be distilled down to two very special travel partners. When you're young, the notion of business travel is envisioned with wide-eyed wonder. The reality is business travel is an endless trek to nowhere. It's a pointless, painful death march, a search for elusive goals and unappreciated successes. For some it is the "A" tour; flying from New York to L.A., or Chicago to Miami.   For me, it was the "C" tour for the most part; driving from Cleveland to Benton Harbor, MI and back with stops in Toledo, OH, Detroit, Cadillac, and Grand Rapids, MI. That kind of windshield time begs for company. It's not that I wasn't successful. That's not the point. It's the amount of time required to accomplish the tasks.

On the plus side, I was blessed to see some amazing sights: moonrises, sunsets, and rainbows. I was able to think, listen to music, eat when and where I wanted. There are some great restaurants out there and some pretty interesting people too. The problem is you're always alone. Keep in mind this is the pre-cell phone era. That's where my wonderful friends and travel companions enter the mix.

I met Grace in nineteen eighty-one. I had just started a new job in a company where we were the only minorities. She was supervisor of accounts receivable. We didn't hit it off right away, but she did give me some good advice on how to get along in my new environment. She was young, beautiful, shapely and incredibly headstrong. Her intelligence and strong will are what the meat of this story is about. However, in the meantime we made friends. Not terribly close mind you. I liked her a lot, but she kept me and probably most people just on the edge of her circle. I don't mean to accuse her of anything, but she was a master of mood swings and manipulating situations. Deep down she was a sweetheart, but she would never let that secret out of the bag. She presented herself as a challenge, which was very important to me.

My next career move landed me in an entrepreneurial start-up venture with tremendous up-side potential. OK, I promise no more sentences like that one! Well after a very successful first year we expanded. Grace's professionalism and analytical skills were just what my department needed. I also knew that she was unhappy in her current position. In one very short year, she not only had picked up the nuts and bolts of the business, but was mastering the requisite interviewing skills necessary to obtain information from clients over the phone. I felt she was ready to travel with me to increase my productivity.

There was always a fair amount of tension between us; invisible to the casual observer, but very obvious to those who knew us. There was a constant intellectual struggle, fueled by her very competitive nature. This was coupled with a difficult to ignore sexual scrimmage. This emotional cold war was waged between an overtly sexual, though emotionally aloof female and an influenced but principled male, who would not give in to his impulses. The battle was largely silent, but intense and frustrating because both of us were used to having things our own way with the opposite sex. This in no way should be interpreted as an even match. She was killing me, and she knew it. She had many advantages over me; better skills, nothing to lose and frankly, she just didn't give a damn. She had mastered a completely beguiling blend of sexuality, coyness, flirtatiousness and distance. She kept me on an emotional rocking horse.

On the day in question we disagreed about lunch. I wanted to drive straight thru to our next appointments that were about eighty-five miles away. She wanted to have lunch first. I finally compromised; stopping at a fast food restaurant to freshen up, pick up lunch and keep going, eating in the car. While I was in the restroom, she ordered lunch and passive aggressively sat down to eat. Not only did she enjoy a leisurely lunch; she then insisted on smoking a cigarette, then two as the snow picked up from flurries to a much heavier pace. Fuming silently, I was intent on making up time to get to our appointments.

After fifty quick miles, especially considering the conditions, we were climbing to the summit of a rare hill when through the heavy snow there was a wall of taillights. Quickly, but gently slowing the car to a stop, I pulled to the side of the road. Unable to see ahead of us on the incline, and with traffic building quickly behind us; we settled in for a long wait. The pace of the snow picked up rapidly, quickly blanketing the car. It had been a half an hour, when I went to the trunk to get the emergency blankets. This proved to be a much more difficult task than I had planned. It was virtually impossible to stand, let alone walk between the gale force winds, blinding snow and treacherous to walk on road conditions.

Having just settled back in the car we heard the roar of a helicopter. Over the next hour we counted five more. We looked at each other and without saying a word, she reached out to hold my hand. We both knew that her insolence had at minimum kept us out of harm's way, and possibly saved our lives.

The freeway opened after almost a three hour wait, and after slowly climbing the snow and ice covered summit we were horrified by the almost surreal sight. The road was strewn with vehicles for miles. We counted thirty seven cars and trucks by the side of the road, in the median. There was evidence that vehicles had gone over embankments and through guardrails. It was a horrible sight. That night we had a great dinner. The mood was much lighter than normal. The three hour dinner was part business, but mostly a celebration of life. She was beautiful, flirtatious and not coy or distant. The remainder of the trip was remarkably civil. She didn't even curse me when I called her room at six-fifteen one morning to tell her to look at the sunrise over the ice floe on the St. Clair River. To this day, she still remembers the beauty of that scene.

# Travel Companions

## Cassie

Cassie was a professional; in fact she was one of the best sales-persons I ever saw. She interviewed for a position on my growing staff and knew more about our service at the end of the day than did our existing staff. She was a natural. She was persistent without being overbearing; inquisitive and probative, but not to the point of annoyance. She was confident enough to ask for the sale; and wily enough to make you think it was your idea. These attributes combined with hard work, enthusiasm and integrity made her an excellent salesperson and worthy adversary to the existing all male staff. In fact, they respected her ability so much that after being hired in April, no one complained when she emerged as the year to date sales leader by September.

However, it must be noted that she also possessed tools in her tool box that no one else had. When she prospected on the phone her voice was like that of a siren's; luring unsuspecting future clients to her shore. When cold calling in person; the object is to get an audience with a decision maker in the company. Not an easy task. But when you have what we dubbed "no appointment legs" the task was considerably easier. On one visit; I actually heard an executive's gatekeeper's reply to her boss' rather terse reply over the phone of "I don't have time to see anyone". She glanced again at Cassie's strong, but feminine crossed legs and said knowingly, "you're going to want to make time for this one". If she got in to see someone it was no contest. Her eyes lit up like the headlights on a car that was racing its engine, as she talked about the service she truly believed in. Then they adopted a fawn-like softness, while she listened to the helpless clients' objections, as she handed them the contract to sign. The women who weren't jealous of her actually applauded. However, I think her best asset was her ability to assess how men thought and adjust her approach accordingly.

One client insisted that we take a plant tour on our impromptu sales call. This was a normal procedure for me on a second visit after receiving information from the client; so that I could prepare and ask pertinent questions. It was rare that sales people were asked to go at all, but upon reaching the shop floor I suspected the reason why. Evidently, so did Cassie.

The only safe way to view the production flow was from the catwalks above the floor. These could only be reached by a series of ladders and open metal staircases. Cassie was wearing a grey pinstripe business suit with a skirt that looked shorter than it was, accented by pumps that OSHA would never approve. Cassie was about five foot six inches tall, but she possessed the legs of a much taller woman and a figure that closely resembled Barbie's.

Upon reaching the first ladder, there was a buzz of anticipation in the assembled group of production supervisors summoned for the tour. Cassie turned to me and winked; I knew at that point that the situation was under control. Here's a point that most women may not know about most men. We would rather catch a glimpse of what you don't want us to see, rather than ogle what you do want us to see. I guess it has something to do with the fruit of the forbidden tree. Without hesitation, Cassie raises the somewhat confining skirt a couple of inches and starts up the ladder. After she clears four or five stairs, I start up after her. Then just as she hears silence from the group below; realizing she has their undivided attention, she nonchalantly calls down to the group in an enchanting non-threatening voice. Without taking her eyes from the ladder, she says "They're burgundy gentlemen". Are you coming up?" Having been totally disarmed, the tour continued without incident. There are many more stories about just how striking a woman she was, even though her real "beauty" was expressed in her genuine kindness and warmth.

I was sent to pick up Cassie from the airport in Indianapolis. We both needed to be in a meeting the following day. I was in Ft. Wayne at the time, so it was a bit out of the way. That wasn't the problem. The problem was incomplete information. I didn't know where to pick her up. After parking the car; I found "Arrivals", picked a concourse and started walking. Frustration was beginning to set in when in the distance I heard a booming male voice. "Damn!" The voice said. Following the voice was the sound of a crash, and the scream of a woman. It seems that a golf cart used to transport passengers had run into a column. I chuckled to myself, knowing that Cassie's flowing sandy to ginger brown hair and long legs couldn't be far behind.

Cassie's powers also extended to women as well. She often was able to extract favors from female employees that were normally reserved for males. They seemed to identify with her struggles to make it in a male dominated field. Of course her appeal wasn't the exclusive domain of men. A waitress once made a rather clumsy overture for her affection, without flinching she ordered the halibut, smiled and stated that she would be (enter your favorite explicative for "sleeping with" here) the gentleman this evening, as she patted the back of my hand. I wished that it were true, silently.

The days on the road were long ones, not counting the lonely hours I spent working in my room in the evenings. My companions had to be much more than associates for me to be successful. They were also excellent conversationalists, singers, comedians and most importantly listeners. These stories take place during one of my longest separations. The road was both solace and torturer. I needed both the money and the work to keep busy; keeping my mind busy made me the most productive that I had ever been. The ladies also provided me with many, but not all of the perks of female companionship with very few of the drawbacks. I owe them a tremendous debt of gratitude for being there for what I needed, when I needed it. We worked very hard and made a lot of money. But most of all; I forged a bond with them that was hardened by the trials of being on the road together, while all the time and tenderness kept it malleable. We were many hours more than friends; seconds from lovers, and light years from being mere co-workers.

Both of them have earned advance degrees and well deserved successes since those days. The best part of all is that after twenty years, I still call them friends. Cassie still holds my hand whenever we're together; a habit she started after my divorce, because I always comforted her during thunderstorms.

Chapter Eighteen

First Dates

Silk


I sat in my office on a beautiful fall afternoon mindlessly working on a computer spreadsheet. It wasn't important or time sensitive work, but it achieved the desired results. My mind only occasionally drifted from the task; keeping me from probing all the possibilities of my new life. My life was being turned upside down by my pending divorce. Never before had I felt this way. My marriage had endured arguments, accusations, separations and reconciliation in the past, but the end had finally come. I felt numb.

My phone rang. Shaking away the cobwebs, I answered in my normal business demeanor. The honey-dipped voice on the other end of the line was confusing to me, professional but friendly, serious yet playful, most importantly familiar, but as of yet unrecognizable. The voice was soliciting a donation for the March of Dimes by asking me to bail the yet to be identified form that owned that beautiful voice out of mock jail. The voice painted a grim picture of her fate that coerced a donation of $100.00 from me. When the name of the organization she represented was revealed the picture became crystal clear. She was the better half of a married couple whom I had sold a house a few years ago. I had barely noticed her as a woman at the time for many reasons, but she seemed very different now. Confident, flirty, professional, and persuasive, a more polished mature version of the woman I remembered. My silence and daydreaming had given her the correct impression that I wasn't quite sure to whom I was speaking. She said, "My name is…."
And from that second forward, I heard her name in every beautiful thing that God's green earth had to offer.

We bade each other well in our careers. She thanked me again for the donation and paused. She said, "I'd like to ask you a big favor. I've just received a big promotion". I interrupted to congratulate her. "I've always admired your business savvy. I was wondering if I could call on you now and again for advice" she asked tentatively. I told her that I was flattered and I would be honored to help her in any way possible. Little did I know that I had just opened the portal to the greatest experience in my already eventful existence.

I was elated to receive a card from her organization. Upon opening it, I discovered a warm handwritten thank you card. She also apologized for not getting back to me personally, realizing she had played heavily on our earlier business transaction, but enjoyed the conversation and hoped the renewed relationship could blossom. This was the first of many such letters and cards that I received from her during our relationship.

I picked up the phone to call her and wish her Happy Holidays. I was disappointed primarily by addressing her answering machine, and secondarily by the lack of a return call. I didn't have time to dwell upon it however; I had some important issues of my own to deal with. By mutual consent the court date for the divorce had been put off until after the holidays; for the sake of the children, but now the day of reckoning was rapidly approaching. The thought of moving in the dead of winter was not appealing to me, but there was no getting around it.

It was a bright, but cold day in early March. I sat in my office watching squirrels playing in the woods. I had been a single man for about one hour. My ex-wife had long since moved out with the children, half of the furniture and most of the money. But most importantly, I had won joint custody of the children. As I watched nature unfold from my window, I thought of the coming of spring, setting up a home, mating… I realized that I needed to get busy finding another place to live. The house had been sold, it was time to go. I dreaded the process of looking for a home alone, full of sadness. Just then the phone rang, I gathered myself, silently mouthing the word "Showtime". I uttered my usual business greeting. The voice on the other end was timid, smaller, and less confident than before. She apologized for not getting back to me sooner but… The silence prompted me to ask, "What was wrong?" It seemed that she needed my advice on how to handle a two-career household. As she spoke, she confessed that both she and her husband had overreacted. She needing better balance; he more understanding. She remembered that I had been separated when I sold them their house. As far as she knew, we had reconciled and moved on. Sensing that I wasn't getting the entire story, I took a deep breath and said "I don't want to take sides in this matter, but I will say that in every marital dispute there are always three sides, his, yours and the truth." She blurted "he thinks I don't have a point; that's why I left him and filed for divorce". She began slowly, but soon a river of pain flowed from her lips as she described the struggles in her marriage. I listened, personalized and identified with her stories. I was so involved in the emotions she described that I almost didn't hear her say; "Do you think my marriage is salvagcablc?" I paused, chose my words carefully and told her that any situation is salvageable. The real question is "Will you like what you'll have after the compromises you'll make to save it". Only you can make that determination. Then she asked me the million-dollar question. "Are you glad you saved your marriage?" I confessed that I might not be the best person to ask, as I had gotten divorced just that morning. "Really…?" She said with more than a little interest in her voice. Then after a long pause, she said we should talk again, and that I had been a great help to her.

I was disappointed that she hadn't asked me any questions about how I felt about my divorce, but I figured she was preoccupied with her own situation. However, I was intrigued by the way she said "really". I tried not to make a lot of it, but her words were still rambling around in my head a couple of days later when the phone rang again, and upon picking up the receiver I heard. "Hello Jim, I hope I haven't caught you at a bad time". She said, assuming I knew who it was. I assured her that I wasn't terribly busy, and that I was actually having difficulty focusing on my work. "That's interesting since I've also been having a hard time concentrating since our last conversation", she admitted coyly. My ears perked up. My interest in her was growing, but I was reluctant to voice it. She was already winning the relationship chess match, and I was powerless to do anything about it. I was giving up way to much emotional information and collecting none. She had sacrificed her pawn to capture my queen. I didn't like my current position, but I had to admit that she was a worthy adversary. I had to go all out, there wasn't much left to lose, except a chance at an enchanting woman.

My new game plan was put to the test later in that same conversation when I suggested that we meet in person to talk. I ordered the crash team to get the paddles ready when my heart stopped, as I waited for her answer. My thoughts raced as the silence continued. Did I ask to soon? Should I de-emphasize the importance of the request? Clear!! My heart started again as she began her answer. "I would love to go out", she said "Plan something special, I could use a break". "I will get back to you on a date, because it is going to take some planning. I hope you understand; having to get a baby sitter and all". I told her I understood, as my brain slowly returned to life. I was still stuck on I would love to go out. We would have two subsequent conversations to nail down the content, time and date of our first encounter. The tension mounted as we jockeyed both mentally and emotionally for relationship superiority. For the first time in many years, I was hanging on for dear life. It's not that my verbal jabs weren't having a positive effect on her; it's just that she always countered with a surprise knockout punch.

The night of destiny had finally arrived, and I was ready. The plans were perfect, I looked great and I was as nervous as I had ever been before a date. We were having dinner at a local upscale jazz club that I often frequented. As it turned out the location was a wise choice on a night that I was obviously going to need some reinforcement.

I met my date at a predetermined location. All of our plans protected her privacy and isolated her family from her actions. She seemed calm and composed when I approached her car. She was a half-hour late and apologetic, but not overly so. I wasn't disturbed as much as I was more nervous. I had dated during my long marital separations, but this was somehow very different. I was single now, all of my actions were life influencing. She emerged from her car wearing a smile that I'm now certain could cure cancer. It certainly calmed my nerves, a least temporarily. She was taller than I remembered; a good thing. In addition to her smile, she wore a black sweater set, a wool checked 18" slim skirt and black tights with mid-heel t-strap pumps. The pearl necklace was a nice finishing touch. She looked in a word, ravishing. Her form was long, lithe and athletic. Her greeting was warm, but somehow distant. She reached out with both hands and clasped my wrists and flashed that smile. We rode to the restaurant in relative silence and for the first time, I detected a little apprehensiveness on her part. The restaurant was crowded, but my reservation got us in right away. The staff's familiarity with me as a regular customer afforded us celebrity status. A new table was brought in and placed near the stage. I shook hands with two business acquaintances on the way to our table, and waved to a foursome across the room. Her grip on my arm was firm, confident, and not at all clingy. By the time we received our menus two drinks had arrived from friends in the room. The songstress spoke to us on her way off stage. She was an old friend from high school, but my date seemed impressed. She commented on my affable personality. Dinner was excellent, but she ate as though it was her last meal. Small bites, no expression, on other occasions she even used a knife and fork to eat pizza. It was a trait that I would learn to understand. Our conversation was spirited and challenging, but sadly limited to breaks. We decided to go elsewhere for dessert.

Upon reaching the car, she turned to thank me for dinner. Her smile actually eliminated the need for dessert. But the best was yet to come. She reached out to embrace me, a moment I'll never forget. She hugged like a boa constrictor. Not crushing, but a total body hug from ankles to earlobes. She wrapped her long left leg around me locking her hips tighter to me. Her equally long arms slid under my arms and locked over my shoulders. Her face brushed mine as it went by. Our ears seemingly locked as her long fingers massaged the back of my head. She felt and smelled divinely. Neither of us spoke, but my knees were noticeably shaking. Her breathing was growing more rapid and shallow.

In retrospect, the scene at the coffee shop was probably comical. We simply glared at each other until our dessert and coffee arrived. I was torn between her long legs, feminine hands, fluorescent smile and warm brown eyes. I didn't know at the time what she was fixating on, but it really didn't matter. I was smitten.

The food loosened our tongues; we discussed our careers and eventually got around to her impending divorce and subsequent life as a single woman. I told her she had enough income to afford a very nice house. That information seemed to please her. She asked if we could see a house that she could afford on her salary. I told her I could show her a couple this weekend. She wanted to see one then; it wasn't hard to convince me.

I was aware of a cute little house that I knew she would love, and it fortunately was vacant. I was correct. She was giddy; slipping out of her shoes, she ran around the house. I delighted in watching her. She was so graceful. She was so excited that when she looked out of the window trying to see the yard, she bumped her head on a glass shelf. She tried to hide it, but I realized that both her forehead and her ego were hurt. I kissed the former and stroked the latter. She melted. A tear formed in her left eye. I asked if she was still hurt, as I held her around her slim waistline. She replied "I've never had a man care for me so" as she raised her left leg to massage my hip with her left knee. She draped her long arms around my neck and with tear filled eyes and a radiant smile she simply said "thank you".

I suggested we take a look at the master bedroom. I walked behind her as we climbed the stairs. She said, "I feel your eyes on me" without turning, but I could hear the smile in her voice. I admitted that her legs were "amazing" and she replied "look all you want". Again she had won. But I had discovered some chinks in her armor. The master bedroom was perfect for her; plenty of windows and closet space. It also had a skylight. When she discovered it, she sprawled out on the floor to look at the stars. I switched off the light, so she could she them better. She looked even more amazing in the moonlight. Somehow her legs looked longer at that angle. She looked so calm lying there. I practically fell down when that smile asked me to lie down with her. We held hands at our sides for several minutes in silence. Then suddenly, she rolled over on top of me and kissed me; cupping my face in her long slender fingers. "I've wanted to do that all evening", she said. Then pausing she said, "But in my fantasy, I wasn't on top". That remark lit the fuse on a powder keg of passion that led to a "dry run" of things to come. When the heavy breathing stopped we stared into each others' eyes. The stare lasted more than several seconds. I blinked first and lost again. I never knew how important that blink would be.

On the way home she was far more relaxed. She talked freely about her plans for the future as she stretched her legs; her feet resting on the dashboard. I asked tentatively about her immediate social plans, she replied "I'm almost certain that a certain tall, handsome man is in my future"

Sunset

Glorious splashes of brilliant color, a treat to the eye.

A kaleidoscope of emotion; a palette in the sky.

Rapidly dulling hues, hope turned to strife.

The last of love's light through the prism of life.

Approaching darkness permeates your soul,

Loving heart made dormant by the accompanying cold.

Passion and memories stored in a safe place.

Loneliness and despair apparent on your face.

The absence of light, definition of doom,

Infinite night surrounds you like an endless room.

The appearance of stars breaks up the dark,

Their flickering glow gives your wounded heart a spark.

Just enough current to help you smile through the pain.

Your mind won't let you believe you've spent love in vain.

Then faintly you hear yourself utter that tired refrain.

Soon the light comes. I'll try love again.

James Robert Russell

# Chapter Twenty

## A Perfect End to a Very Long Day

She walked in the door; her usual bright spirit dulled by the abuses of the day. As she flopped on the couch without speaking; I knew that the situation was urgent and required my immediate attention. I offered her a drink and asked her how her day had been. She barely responded. I removed her shoes and massaged her feet, while urging her to continue to talk. I was able to raise her feet and lie her down. As I stroked her head, I realized that I was not having much success. Nor had the wine had a noticeable effect. I continued to talk to her hoping my voice would soothe her, as I worked my way down her body, being careful not to linger in any particular area. As I sat at her feet; wondering what to do next, I was overwhelmed by her beauty. Her body was rigid with anxiety, but her lovely form was still lithe and feminine. She subconsciously called out for help, belying her exterior demeanor. I wanted to be closer; to take away her pain. At the same time, the need to be close to her heated up my passion. She spoke vaguely, and as I asked her more questions to keep her talking, I raised her legs to my shoulders. She stopped talking, noticing the changed look on my face. I kissed the inside of her ankle. She gave me the mixed message of a partial smile, while shaking her head. Undeterred, I continued to kiss her legs ever so gently, as she continued to speak. Her words came to her easier now; more fluent and determined. I inched ever so slowly up her legs, relishing the silky feeling of her legs on my cheeks and lips. By now, her speech had slowed. She playfully asked me what I was doing, showing me the first sign of recovery.

She didn't want to respond, but she had to admit that he had gotten her attention. The paralyzing tension she felt when she came home was slowly being replaced by different energy. She felt his lips so gently on her thighs. She began to feel compassion for him as she looked down at him. The love he felt for her permeated her skin with each caress. His love filled her soul, lifted her spirits, totally replacing the heaviness and gloom of the day. Without speaking, she removed his shirt, mostly for her own benefit, to see his back as he worked his magic. She also knew he loved her touch. He had told her many times of the feelings her silky legs around him stirred. "The shape and movement of her legs were the essence of femininity". Remembering the sound of the words; the passion in his voice, left no doubt about the depth of his love for her.

Sensing her increasing involvement, I reached up and carefully, slowly, and gently tugged at her panties. I kept the same pace of my kisses. The feel of her panties accelerated the fire that was my passion. The panties slid off effortlessly, and as they left her ankles I was able to look at her in total for the first time. I was mesmerized by the vision in front of me. Lovely long silken legs encased in nylon, topped by lace. Her skirt barely covered her pubic hair, and left a portion of one cheek exposed. I only glanced at her momentarily, although it seemed like an eternity. As I resumed my caresses, starting again at the ankles. I noticed her mood was completely different. The rigidness was gone; her breathing that previously was heavy with the weight of her problems was now deeper and freer flowing. My kisses were now accompanied by licks and nibbles. Her emotional changes were now affecting me, as I worked my way up her thigh. I could feel her alternating between muscle tension and relaxation. Her heart rate increased, while her breathing became more rapid and shallow. As I drew even closer, the heat of her passion was more evident. She slightly opened her legs, raising the humidity level. Her movement also revealed to me for the first time her feminine essence. Her scent was intoxicating. The unmistakable sweet aroma that IS woman. The pulsating layers of womanhood were just an inch from my face. I was in heaven. I paused to take it all in.

She wondered why he waited; she looked at herself wrapped around him. His head was poised between her legs. She truly felt loved at this moment, so individually special. The singular focus of her lover's attention. Her body was overwhelmed with emotion at this point. Her mind still full of her problems, her body filling with passion. Still, she wondered why he waited. Did she do something wrong? Did he change his mind?

She wanted to do the right thing. The ladylike thing, but his hot breath between her legs clouded her judgment. She caressed his head, her passion building. Suddenly, she stopped thinking. Her passion was getting the best of her. She hoped to do the right thing, but she really no longer cared. When her body could hold no more; she revealed herself, simultaneously opening her legs and forcing his head between them. When his lips met hers she erupted like a volcano. She felt passion, lust, power, love and release. She looked down at him and panicked. How did he take it? What was he thinking? Almost immediately, she got her answer. The muscles of his neck, back and shoulders flexed, as he settled in to his task.

I was energized by her show of passion, and resolved to do my best to please her. Not a difficult task however, since it was so enjoyable. As I licked and kissed her femininity ever so gently, exploring her creases and folds. I felt her body slowly relaxing. Each part of her body was drained of its grief individually, from the top of her head downward. Her agony was being siphoned from her body into my waiting mouth. Her tension and pain electrified me. Her lightened body began to respond to me, her slowly undulating hips pumping out her problems. The most intimate of connections was benefitting us both. Her anxiety was now completely eliminated; allowing her passion to rise. It raced through her like a wildfire, her body moving wildly to the probing of my tongue.

She looked down on him between uncontrolled panting breaths, noticing the dampness at her forehead. She flung her head back to fully enjoy the moment. When her glance returned to him tirelessly pleasing her, she realized what it was all about. She understood the devotion, the selflessness, the passion. She then wanted him to experience through her, the feelings he aroused in her. She diverted her energy from her brain, and succumbed to her emotions. She grabbed his empty hands and filled them with her breasts. The bond was exhilarating. When he applied the proper pressure, she returned her hands to his head holding him firmly to her now uncontrolled bucking hips. Instantly, she felt a level of passion never before attained. The heat from a fire that she never allowed herself to feel. She floated and soared. Her emotions were at their lifetime peak. She was about to explode.

I was amazed at this new level of passion, it made me more determined to take her to the limit. I drank from her now dripping valleys, lapping up my rewards. I knew the climax was near, as she grabbed my head the second time. I was honored to share this journey with her. Then suddenly it happened. She emitted a low moan. It was a primal, guttural utterance that sounded as if had been trapped for a very long time. Then came the initial clench of her thighs around my ears, toes gripping my back, velvet-like pubic hair on my cheek, her essence in my mouth. She jerked three more times in rapid succession. Finally, she exhaled, releasing a lifetime of repression. Her body slowly relaxed, with me licking her slowly, easing her down.

When she had eased the grip of her thighs, I rubbed my face in her juices, filling my pores with her essence, bonding us even further. I raised my head to look at her as a single tear formed in her left eye. We kissed gently at first; then heatedly, passionately. We had reversed roles, her tongue probing the recesses of my mouth, now flavored by the sweet taste of her essence.

As she kissed him, her nostrils filled with the smell of her womanhood. She now understood the attraction, the way she made him feel. She showed her appreciation and approval by licking his love stained face. She laid back to rest and returned his head to its place. She felt so free, so relaxed. She was physically naked, his face being her only cover. But more importantly, she knew his emotional bond was her armor. Life would never get to her again.

I never felt so close to anyone before. What we had shared had transcended the physical. We had formed a union that would fortify us forever.

As they dozed off to sleep, they dreamed of the future, their future. They slept the way only lovers sleep. The relaxing, rejuvenating controlled coma that lifts the spirit and bonds the soul.


James Russell

A Day in Love's Journey

The mere hint of the dawn, a faint glow in the distance illuminates the dark corners where the demons of despair reside. The slowly brightening sky raises hopes, while streaks of vivid pastels energize the spirit. The newborn daylight reveals the damage of the night. The ravaged heart and soul lay flattened and shredded like freshly mowed grass by the bitter cruelty of past lost loves. Tears of pain and loneliness lay in miniature pools, like dew on the deflated and desolate heart.

Undaunted, the warmth of the early morning sun reminds the patient of pleasures gone by, while slowly erasing the horrors of the past. Evaporating those memories in a soul cleansing haze; allowing clear vision once again. Radiating warmth loosens fear frozen arms, allowing access to the heart and the ability to reach out to that special someone again.

The midday sun revives the passion, that white-hot intensity that melds two hearts, minds and souls into one powerful alloy. Unique as the newly joined lovers, this unified strength will weather the battles of life. Ward off the advances of love starved suitors, and all others bent on the destruction of their harmony.

The late afternoon heat brings the inevitable storms, furious battles with rain, wind and hail meant to test the depth and breathe of their love. Their surface may show the scars of the journey, but the pits, scratches, and slightly dulled finish belies the underlying strength of their conviction.

The developing surface rust matches the patina of the early evening sun. A symbol of the changing, but not diminishing affection shared by two. Fading light only reminds them of the importance of the remaining time, as the brilliant red of the waning sun mimics their lifelong love affair now glowing red-hot, like embers in a fireplace. Only time can end this bond, as the light of one or both finally goes out. Leaving only the warmth of the ash in remembrance of the passion, love and devotion they shared.

Passionately remitted, to Lizzy my one and only love.


James Robert Russell

# Chapter Twenty-Two

## The Clock Struck Twelve

A major metropolitan city was the backdrop for their incredible evening. He had planned perfectly. Horse drawn carriage to the theater where they were transformed by an amazing presentation of the Phantom. Afterwards, they dined in a nearby New York style bistro. The restaurant's mahogany wood trim and cozy leather booths provided warmth, while the garnet colored walls picked up and magnified the fiery glow from the candleholders, which provided the majority of the light in the room. The tables were adorned with oversized, starched, white linen table cloths. Perfect for concealing under the table activities. That is if they were interested in hiding. Their passion was fueled by veal chops, lobster tails and probably one too many bottles of wine. They laughed, talked, teased and pleased, as they fed each other tiramasu.

She returned from the ladies room delicate panties in hand, his reward for practically undressing her during dinner. She had discovered early in the relationship, that she enjoyed being disrobed in public as least as much as he enjoyed seeing her. She strode confidently, yet ever so gracefully toward him, her panties dangling from a single slender finger. His mind wandered, remembering how time had stood still at the theater. She stood at the top of the grand spiral staircase, her graceful swan-like neck framed beautifully in the high collar of her designer dress. It was as if she were the only woman in the room. Her athletically feminine form seemingly floating down the stairs, parting the sea of obviously inferior women. Her eyes met mine, as she scanned the lobby. Her smile had an infrared effect, warming me from across the room. The crowd responded as though they had seen royalty, as she took my arm and glided toward the auditorium. They had received this type of treatment before. In every city that they had visited, their dapper forms had garnered celebrity type attention. In St. Louis, for example their late night promenade from a restaurant to a night club was accompanied by applause and stopped traffic. Perhaps they deserved the attention, he a full 6'8" and she standing a bit over 6' in heels. They strolled in timelessly elegant, designer evening wear against the backdrop of a much too casual world. It must have truly been a sight to see.

Her perfume awakened him in time to hear the giggle, as she walked past him. She looked back and beckoned him as she obviously stuffed the small silk panties into his hand. The staff had been well compensated for their attentive, yet invisible service, as they had stayed open well past their normal closing. Their faces revealed the fact that they would have settled for watching that backless silk crepe dress leave the restaurant.

The early autumn night had just the hint of a chill. He gallantly removed his jacket, and in a flourish placed it about her shoulders. She melted into his arms caressing his Egyptian cotton clad chest. His heart accelerated and the custom garment filled with the expansion of his lungs. She cooed when she noticed that the fine English wool of his French tailored pants was having difficulty containing his now granite-like manhood. Pressing herself against him, she reached up and around his neck to kiss him. In doing so, she exposed her entire lower half to him; while still covered by his jacket. She had accomplished her goal of being naked in the streets.

Holding her revealed just how tough of a task her dress had, just to be as soft as her skin. He remembered why he had given her the name of Silk. Originally, the inspiration for the name was the softness of her trademark silk stockings that she always wore. He also recalled his disappointment earlier in the evening when she appeared not wearing them. She broke the kiss saying "I love it when you treat me like a lady" with a sly sarcastic smile, as the dress fell back to its burden of hugging her silken curves. She walked away, her stilettos making just the slightest impact on the pavement. Her feet held in sexual bondage by straps that can only be mastered by the Italians.

He remembered the last time he had heard those words. It was earlier this evening in their box at the theater. She had been guiding his hand up and down her legs. Her skin was supple and completely hairless. By the middle of third act her dress was around her waist. She was alternately pushing his fingers inside her, and sucking on the previously used digits. His hand almost completely inside her, she leaned over and whispered in his ear "I love it when you treat me like a lady." She had said the same thing, later in the restaurant when she had dared him to undo the single button on the collar of her dress, allowing complete access to and view of her breasts. He responded by saying "later", while sliding his hand across her back and inside her dress, cupping and squeezing her firm breasts, while she fed him dessert.

She loved the way he looked at her. Also the way he allowed her to freely express her sexuality. He transported her to emotional places she never knew existed. His touch kept her moist at all times. She was aroused by even his phone calls and notes. She motioned him over to her at the fountain.

She was beautiful. Her form was accentuated by shadow and moonlight, which paled in comparison to her smile. He remembered from his earlier expeditions and her silky gift, that she was now completely naked under her minimal silken drape.

The spray from the fountain was chilly, but arousing. He reached her just as the bell in the church tower began to strike twelve. There were only a few people left on the square at this hour. She overwhelmed by the moment; struck at the third bell. Neither of them had any idea that she was turned on by getting wet. The fountain had started a chain reaction in her that she was powerless to stop. The volcano that had been building inside her all evening was about to erupt. She had been careful not to have an orgasm all evening. But not even she could have predicted what was about to happen.

She climbed on the edge of the pool and leapt into his arms. She wrapped her now bare lower torso around him, kissing him passionately. The long, powerful and graceful legs that had given her the advantage in college sports now had the advantage over him. The fountain's cold spray on her buttocks only made her hotter.

He stumbling from the suddenness of her advance began to fall. She landed in the fountain, her passion dragging him in as well. They kissed again; now completely drenched. He lifted and swung her out of the fountain as the clock struck nine. They ran laughing across the street toward their hotel and through the lobby in the direction of the elevators.

The look on her face was unlike any he had ever seen. She panted, laughed and stared. Passion oozed from every pore. He sensing the moment snatched the dripping jacket from her and said "later", as he pushed her into the elevator and undid the button on her collar. Her fountain drenched dress fell to the floor, as the elevator doors closed.

She exploded. She was now completely naked. Her beautiful body was restrained by only those tiny Italian straps. She dropped to her knees ripping his pants down. She quickly shoved him down her throat, experiencing her first orgasm. As she recovered, the city's skyline came into view. It was a glass elevator! She was reinvigo-rated by the realization of one of her fantasies. She had always wanted to suck him in public. She grabbed him, forcing him ever deeper down her throat. Each of his gagging thrusts reinforced her initial orgasm. She wanted to drain him. To have an audience watch her swallow his nectar, but it was not to be. She felt her head jerk back.

He had grabbed her by the hair and pushed her against the glass. Her face and breasts were smashed against the glass. She had awakened the animal in him. She was terrified and delighted at the same time. The pain of each thrust was wonderful. She was being fucked by a madman in front of an entire city! She thought. Why couldn't the doors open so someone could get a closer view?! As the elevator reached the top floor, she tried to get away, only to be grabbed by an ankle. He tripped and fell on her, as his pants were still around his ankles. As he wrestled to get his pants off, she jumped on him, rolling him over. She hurt herself riding him. Each painful thrust proved his dominance over her and brought her closer to her third climax. After reaching the summit for the third time and still feeling the energy of the throbbing force inside of her, she rolled off of him exhausted and simply said "do what you will with me." Dragging her into the hallway, he mounted her; throwing her legs over his shoulder. She enjoyed lying there helpless being thoroughly probed, feeling his tremendous passion with each poke in her diaphragm. She loved the way he savagely chewed on her breasts before he flipped her over bringing her to her fourth orgasm, as she was ground into the carpet.

Finally, he gently placed on her back and reentered her. This time he slowly and deeply stroked her. She looked up to watch him entering her repeatedly. Amazed and revived by the intimate scene, she summoned all her remaining strength and began to buck her hips. Sensing his imminent orgasm, she screamed "fill me up baby." As he obeyed her command, partially inside as well as on her, as was his custom, a single tear formed and rolled from her left eye.

She had been publicly idolized, loved, and screwed. All of her fantasies had been fulfilled at once. What was most important to her was that she had experienced his tremendous passion for her. She had never felt so loved. She saw the confused look on his face when he saw the tear. She simply said "thank you" and slid her head under his hips for a final time. She loved to chew on his now limp manhood. Sucking the last of his nectar from him, she mixed the taste of his passion with hers.

He helped her up and watched her stagger exhausted, naked and beautiful down the hallway, dragging her dress behind her. As she leaned on the door of their hotel suite, striking a pose that reflected what she had just been through. She looked back at him, smiled and said in her sexy, sultry voice. "You do want seconds, don't you?"

# Letters

## Silk I

I once wrote about a woman, a woman whose incredibly soft texture and gentile manner belies a tougher internal fiber. I fell in love with that beautiful woman and nicknamed her Silk. In the two plus years since that time I've become more intimately involved with the woman that so closely reminds me of that mysterious, indescribable, irresistible fabric.

I've had the opportunity to experience a kaleidoscope of emotions, feelings and expressions. The warmth of her eyes and engaging smile calls to mind the feel of raw silk. The casual comfort and versatility she exudes always provides me with a sense of purpose and belonging. Her voice floats to my consciousness, as if carried on a tropical breeze. The sheer fabric of its timber and inflection elevates my temperature, while at the same time teasing my libido and uplifting my spirit with its effervescence.

She has woven a colorful emotional tapestry; the effect of its vibrancy and subtle nuances on me is dramatic and long-lasting.

I can only describe the feeling she gives me as being "touched by a web". A web, that whispery combination of sensory impulses. Woven expertly by a maestro of seemingly the flimsiest of materials. However, the web possesses the power to support, protect and provide nourishment. All this accomplished while being virtually invisible. In my case, Silk provides me with support for and nourishment of my hopes, dreams and aspirations. She gives structure to my life, simultaneously insuring stability, as well as freedom. This loving environment bonds without binding. This attitude can only foster personal growth and deepen our commitment to each other.

I relish in the thought of being draped in the fabric that makes it possible for me to be the person that I've always wanted to be. I can only hope that in return, the person that I will become will provide the love of my life everything she needs to grow and prosper. As she has done for me.

Love Always,


Jim

Some of the most memorable parts of an intimate relationship are the little things that only the two of you know. The thoughts, jokes and games you play. This is one of those tongue in cheek communications we shared. Let your imagination run free!

Job Posting – Open Interviews

Master Carpenter's Assistant

Requirements:

Must be skilled, novices need not apply. Flexible schedule, occasional long or odd hours will be required. Frequent jobs to be performed at a moment's notice. Experience needed in both digital and manual hammering. Ability and willingness to perform tasks on all types of flooring, including tongue in groove. This is not a management position, must be willing to work under or over master carpenter as requested. Must be able to work in tight places, sunlight and dark, indoors and out in all types of weather. Must perform both public and private sector jobs.

Many interviews will be required; several oral and field tests will be given. Applicant must have suitable wardrobe, and may be asked to work with or without uniform on request. Successful applicant should have large appetite, as master carpenter will supply abundant and frequent hot meals. Must be self-starter and energetic, but willing to follow directions to a tee. Rewarding position for the right applicant.

Apply in person

# The Repo Man

Come to collect on an overdue debt. What you owe is some love.
Need to get inside you; fit like a glove.

Wanna suck on your lips, while you're rolling those hips. Hold
your hands down while I lick down south; then climb up on top
and fuck you in the mouth.

Take you on a picnic; have big fun. Good music, food and making
love in the sun.

You wear something hot to our cozy little spot. You put my hand
up your dress, so I can feel what you've got. Romantic mood,
candlelight and your incredible eyes; for dessert I get your luscious
thighs.

On the way out you take my arm, walking so gracefully, overwhelming me with charm. I hear your sweet voice; you touch me
here and there. You give me that look; offer me a dare. You give
me no choice; got me so hot. I bend you over and take you, right
in the parking lot. I take you home; drive real slow. Get you out of
your clothes; see how fast you can go. You flash me that mischie-
vous smile every once in a while, as you tirelessly suck me mile
after mile.

I get you back home, you invite me in. We both fall asleep, wearing only a satisfied grin. We dream of our love complete and deep.
Unconscious, still united in the middle of the night. Without making a sound, we make love in our sleep.

The principal, the basis, is my undying love. The time has come,
the interest is due. The same interest payments I'll make to you.

Being in love's debt; it's a beautiful thing. Like a mortgage; binding till death. The larger the debt, the greater our wealth. I can't wait to sign the papers; give you a ring.

Comment if you care to; act it out if you dare. Written for fun, but backed by serious love.

Jim

## Thinking of You

I chanced upon this poem today; it made me think of you. Your
form, your voice, your sexy ways immediately came to view.

I cannot take credit for writing it. But its words are definitely true.
It describes so accurately; the deep love I have for you.

## Compared

I tried to compare the light of your eyes to that of the stars; but
stopped for fear of making the stars seem less bright.

I tried to compare your voice to that of heavenly music; but
stopped for fear of making music lose its delight,

I tried to compare your presence to that of sunshine's; but stopped
for fear of making the sun lose its heat.

I tried to compare your scent to that of a rose; but stopped for fear
of making the rose smell less sweet.

I tried to compare your passionate spirit to that of fire's; but
stopped for fear of putting out heat's only flame.

I tried to compare your beauty to that of an angel; but stopped for
fear of putting the angel to shame.

By Travis Bennett

Chapter Twenty-Seven

Letters

Silk II

My Dearest Silk,

I write to you in an attempt to explain and clarify what I am thinking and feeling about my life as it currently is, and what I hope it
will be. I believe that there are critical points in a person's life that
define their level of success and happiness. The decisions at these
critical moments should be given careful consideration. This is one
of those moments for me.

During the last two and one-half years, I have been bombarded
with a number of potentially devastating situations. I have been
emotionally stressed, financially strained and in constant physical
pain. I have survived these times through the grace of God, whose
compassion has provided me with the love of a good woman,
the blessing of good friends and an indomitable spirit. I have not
always passed the tests that have been put to me, but they all have
served as a learning experience. How my recent experiences and
tests have affected me and my future is what I write to tell you.

In the second half of my life, I am in the process of developing
some principles and practices that will enhance the quality and
happiness of my life along, with the lives of the people I touch.
They are planning, patience and passion.

Planning – The importance of planning cannot be under-estimated.
You can never eliminate all of the potential pitfalls in life, but you
can through careful comprehensive planning minimize the number
of, or the effect of these events. It is the only non-emotional part
of my being. It is however, very important in my overall emotional
stability. Through the solid efforts based on an innovative plan, all

of our dreams can be realized. Strategy will provide some of the most important aspects of comfortable stress-free existence. Proper planning maximizes the output of labor, which in turn reduces the amount of effort; while increasing profit and leisure time. Spontaneity, the spice of life is a product of planning and time management. Please note: creativity, innovation and spontaneity are very important in a personal relationship. They are not mechanical operations, as you well know. But when life is dictated by the demands of work or lack of efficiency, then the result is emotional monotony.

Monotony breeds boredom with a relationship and in life. Out of boredom comes despair about a person's future; and we both know where that leads. I have not changed my outlook or expectations about my life. Moreover, I have not given up on my lofty goals of personal achievement. But my primary goal; my yardstick of achievement will be happiness in and success of my personal relationships. Without them life is meaningless.

Patience – I'd like to think that patience has always been one of my strengths. It has increased with age and experience, but now a higher level and greater scope is needed. Patience is not simply a willingness to wait. It is a combination of confidence in oneself, compassion for others, the willingness to change and most importantly acceptance of a higher power. The last point is obvious and self evident, so I will concentrate on the others. If you have done all you can do with a situation in life, (i.e. planned, thought out, implemented and followed-up) that knowledge gives you confidence. Apprehension is borne out of the lack of control of your options. If you still have options available to you, it means that you have not controlled your own destiny.

That lack of control is a breeding ground for fear and apprehension. More importantly, it causes you to make irrational decisions and behave erratically. The effect of that behavior on the people around you is devastating. It leaves them uncertain and insecure about their future. Avoiding this effect on others is my primary motivation in achieving this goal.

Passion - One of the definitions of passion is the intensity at which you live your life. I strive to find joy in even the simplest tasks that must be performed. Passion determines to a great degree how successful one will be at a given task, because it determines how much of yourself that you are willing to risk. This theory applies to both work and play. An example would be a party. Parties are made of hosts/hostesses intent on their guests enjoying themselves, and equally important are guests expecting and willing to contribute to having a good time. In relationships, passion is contagious and nourishing to your partner. The most effective way to invoke passion in someone is to show it. A gift received with enthusiasm will encourage future gift giving.

Support and enthusiasm for the professional endeavors of a partner are nourished by the passion exuded. Everyone wants to be a part of a winning experience. Especially when the winner is someone you love. Without passion we are simply objects to be acted upon. Waiting to be told what to feel, where to go and how to act. This person becomes a burden as one partner is supplying the energy for the both of them.

These are my basic principles for the rest of my life. There are of course many other things affecting my philosophies, which I would love to discuss with you. Additionally, your input and perspective is always welcome and encouraged. Remember, anything we do to enhance a life benefits the other in a loving relationship.


All ideas submitted with respect and love,


Jim

# Chapter Twenty-Eight

## Marcel

It was a particularly low point in my life after the tremendous high of being in a marvelous; albeit tumultuous relationship with Silk. Its implosion sent me spiraling into an abyss; a level of depression that not even I could have imagined. The situation was compounded by the fact that I lived in a community where the nuclear family was king. My sphere of exposure consisted of my children and their friends, the kids I coached, and the parents of both groups, along with my clients and attorneys. None of which were available for dating. It had been just under a year since my last date. I was terribly lonely; so much so that I joined a telephone dating service. I optimistically recorded what I thought was a clever ad and waited for results. Two weeks passed with only minimal and unwanted results. I decided to take control of my own fate. I searched through what seemed like thousands of lost female souls; fast forwarding to the next after only a few seconds of their greeting. I wasn't sure of what I was looking for, but I knew what I didn't want. On the third night of searching, just when I was about to give up in frustration, I heard the "Music". Actually, what she said was "Hello Gentleman". What I heard was class, grace, intelligence, confidence and warmth. Her voice transcended and superseded the words. I left her a message with instructions on how to reach me, and suggested that she listen to my profile to get an idea what she was getting herself into, if she chose to call. I so hoped that she would call back.

The following evening my office phone rang. I answered in my normal business greeting, just in case it was one of my West Coast clients. A warm upbeat voice responded, "Hello Jim, this is Marcel". "I hope this is a good time for you". There was an awkward silence that seemed to be a lot longer than the few seconds it actually lasted. I responded, "Anytime would a good time for you to call," before I thought. I regretted saying it as soon as the words left my mouth. I feared sounding too anxious: desperate. Her alto sonata continued, bailing me out immediately. "I was beginning to lose faith in this system." "I thought I would never find someone that interested me." "Me too," I replied boyishly. "See, that's what I'm talking about." "You have honesty, vulnerability, and confidence." "Someone that doesn't take himself too seriously". We connected immediately.

Our conversation was spirited. Topics ranged from our career choices; through our children, touching on goals and aspirations. She was ambitious but honest; hard working but balanced. Balance seemed to be one of her strengths. She had traveled, appreciated the finer things, but enjoyed equally the simple beauty of nature. Her voice was a symphony. Most people use their voice to impart information. She had elevated conversation to an art form. The combination of diction, inflection and a delightful lilt in her voice expertly conveyed a kaleidoscope of emotions, all while being thoroughly entertaining. I had lapsed into a comfortable trance while listening to her recount the story of her recent move back to northern Ohio when suddenly, abruptly, the music stopped. She warmly and sincerely apologized for taking up so much of my time on a first phone call. She gave me her number and urged me to call her back anytime, and hurriedly hung up the phone. Totally caught off guard, I replayed the conversation in my head. Did I say something to upset her? No. Did I bore her? I didn't think so; I had done most of the listening. The conversation had lasted a little more than an hour, maybe she had something to do or honestly didn't want to take up more of my time. Fifteen minutes passed before I made the bold decision to call her back. With my heart beating like a drum, I reached for the phone, dialed and prayed. I hoped she wouldn't find me pushy or worse, just weird. "Hello, this is Marcel," the voice on the other end of the line said. "I hope you don't mind my calling you back so soon, but I missed you already" I replied, trying to sound as controlled as possible, hoping for the best. I got my answer in a voice as breezy as a day in April. "I hoped you would call back." "I really didn't want to end the conversation, but I had to pee so badly." We both laughed heartily, she from embarrassment, and I from relief and enjoyment of her candor. We talked another two hours until midnight. I thanked her for her time, as we made a date to talk again the next day at 9 pm.

I admitted that, "I had never had so much fun with a woman that I had never met, especially considering I still had my clothes on." "I had a great time too", she said. "I guess it's O.K. for me to admit to you that my panties are wet". Pleased and stunned, but still quick of wit I replied, "Save them for me". She answered quickly, as though she was relieved that her admission had been well received. "I will." "They're pink" "Until tomorrow I crooned." "It's a date," she chirped. Thus was the beginning of a great relationship and a continuing tradition.

The next day flew by in anticipation of again talking with Marcel. The chance meeting of someone so wonderful renewed my hopes of finding my ultimate soul mate. Tonight's conversation would go a long way toward determining how much we really had in common. With the "first date" jitters now out of the way, would the second conversation sputter for energy and die? I certainly hoped that it wouldn't. I was resolved to find out. At minimum, just talking to her had cured months of loneliness. I had suffered through the kind of loneliness that is hard to describe. I was around people and busy all the time. There wasn't time to wallow in self-pity. But there was an acute awareness of the loss of a connection with someone. That direct tie that replenished the soul; challenged the mind, and awakened the senses.

I sat at my desk pretending to prepare for the next day. At 8:58 pm, I picked up the phone and dialed. I could wait no longer. The anticipation was killing me. I hoped she understood my urgent need to talk to her. The phone only rang once. "Jim?" The mellow voice answered with more than a bit of excitement. "Why didn't you call sooner?" My heart jumped. She had a way of making you feel supremely special with just a few words. The second conversation was more animated than the first. It intertwined questions with dialogue. We shared humorous stories and sadness. We discussed our expectations for relationships. Nothing was held back and there were no surprises. In fact, the more we talked I found that there was much more common ground than not. This looked promising.

We relented to the urges of nature at midnight. Our appetites for each other's company had grown to the point that we simply put our phones down and ran to the bathroom; unwilling to risk breaking the connection. We continued on until at 3 am. Exhausted we ended the conversation without making an appointment for our next date.

The fact that we hadn't planned our next conversation weighed heavily on me the next day. A shadow of doubt came over everything we had shared. I thought about the subjects we hadn't talked about. Was the usual curse about to take over? Had the bubble burst? At exactly 1pm, after a client lunch I called her, and left the following message. "I really enjoyed our conversation last night." "You are a tasty little morsel." "But I fear I'll be hungry again tonight around eight". I spent the rest of the day wondering what her response would be to the message when she arrived home from work. I admit I was a little worried. I arrived home after coaching football around 7:30 and non-chalantly checked my messages. Business calls would wait until tomorrow, telemarketing calls deleted. Then I noticed a call that came in at precisely 1pm from a number that I didn't recognize. The surprise of hearing that musical voice forced me to sit. The voice spoke in a tone so sad, that I could barely stand to listen. I felt like a man being read a death sentence. The voice said "Jim, I'm sorry that I didn't promise to call you today. It's been bothering me all day." "I've thought about nothing else. It's hard for me to work. Please call me as soon as you get this message." That message was a defining moment. It was conformation of mutual interest. We were both smitten. I use that old-fashioned term purposefully. We were courting, the way people used to do with letters. We based our feelings on the content of each other's convictions. We were candid, honest and unaffected by the distractions of physicality. Our connection was real and substantial. Our passion was building momentum based on the anticipation of the next response. The foundation for a great and lasting relationship was being built, one marathon conversation at a time.

It had been three weeks since our initial conversation. Our conversations were now less frequent but the passion, enthusiasm and intensity had not waned. The simple fact was we were both exhausted. We had covered nearly everything that a couple can talk about; serious topics, advice sessions, and what I like to call "Seinfeld" calls. The conversation wasn't really about anything, but they were always warm and entertaining. The last conversation devoted a full two hours to sex. That bridge crossed; there were only two things left. We both admitted that the avoidance of the first subject of when and how we would finally meet had been a defensive maneuver. That coupled with the fact that we had never really discussed our respective appearances. She knew that I was tall. I knew she had medium brown eyes. We both now said that we had been called good looking by the opposite sex, but that was of course subjective and open to interpretation. We were entertained by each other's horror stories. The deliberate act of avoiding those last two subjects was an obvious ploy to keep the "fantasy" alive. Marcel suggested that we meet in two weeks. I would plan the dinner date. Together we cooked up the plan that would give each of us an "escape hatch".

We were to meet in a parking lot not far from her home. The instructions were to park on opposite sides of the lot facing the middle, as if we were jousting. On her signal of flashing headlights, we would roll to the center of the lot with our driver's sides closest, to offer each other a clear view of the person whom we had grown so fond. In a perfect world, I'd like to say that it didn't matter how she looked. In some ways it didn't, but we both had such discriminating tastes that frankly it did matter. The emotional build-up had been so great that we were both primed for a huge letdown. You could argue on one hand, that a person that seemed to be so balanced and complete had to have a deficit somewhere. It could be why she had delayed our meeting, so that I could fall for the person that she was inside, with the hope that I could overlook her external image. The theory had merit. She had presented a wonderful internal image. She had integrity, consistency, and intelligence, wit. Loads of charm and compassion. These things took time and effort to develop. A woman that simply focused on her looks; well you've met that type before. On the other hand, could not those attributes be translated to the visual? Remember my definition of beautiful is atypical. Could she not be one of those rare, fortunate creatures that have all the tools? After all, I was. I chuckled to myself.

I was dressed fairly conservatively in a dark charcoal business suit, crisp new white shirt and a patterned burgundy tie. It was my impression that Marcel liked it that way. I believe that a person's wardrobe says a lot about them. My style choices stated clearly timeless, structured, and expensive in a covert way. I was comfortable in my own skin and my clothes were a reflection of that. I wore cologne so that you could tell that I did. But if you wanted to get the full effect you had to come close. It was early autumn and the warm, but early setting sun led to rapid evening cooling. One final look in the vanity mirror. All systems go. As I returned the visor to its closed position, a cool breeze on my slightly moist brow brought me back to consciousness. Just then, the flash of headlights in front of me alerted me to Marcel's arrival. The moment of truth had arrived. I started my car and returned the headlight flash. As I put my car in gear, I recalled the rules. If either of us didn't like what we saw in each other, we could keep on driving with no hard feelings. We moved closer at a crawl. My heart was beating in my chest like a timpani drum. Our cars were side by side and sensory overload caused me to go blank. I only remember the daring look in her eyes and a wry smile as she went by. I stopped. I didn't dare look back, in fear that she was gone. I saw two flashes of red taillights in my driver's side mirror, and my heart restarted. That was the signal of approval.  I put the car in reverse to finally meet Marcel in person. I put the car in park and looked at her fully for the first time. She was a classic beauty in café au lait. She wore her hair in a complex looking up do. Her warm brown eyes possessed a challenging character. As I stood to my full height and walked to her car, she seemed to be non-chalantly sizing me up. She exited the car just as I reached her vehicle. She was of average height, about 5'6" tall. She wore a stylishly simple black crepe dress, black hose and mid-heel suede pumps. A burgundy paisley scarf was worn as a shawl.

There were no outrageous features about her, just a perfect size 6. She took my arm as I walked her back to my vehicle. She had a way of making you feel good with a small gesture as well. I opened the passenger door and she entered; sitting and turning with both knees and ankles together, while only momentarily removing her eyes from my face. Perfect! By the time I got behind the wheel, she had found the single rose I had purchased for her. "For me?" she asked with both lips and eyes. I responded, "Had I known that you were going to smell so good, I would have gotten a scentless variety of flower". This time a single raised eyebrow accompanied her mysterious glance. I thought to myself; I made a couple of points with that remark. I think. I put the car in gear and exited the parking lot. Upon reaching the freeway entrance ramp, I thanked her for coming. She seemed genuinely touched by that remark, but said nothing. As we merged onto the freeway I said, "I think you'll really enjoy the restaurant." "I'm sure I will" she replied, looking at me fully. "You seem to have very good taste". With my right hand on the console, I extended my pinkie finger in her direction. She put the rose in her right hand and without speaking locked the pinkie finger of her left hand around mine. Perfect!

The remainder of the ride was in relative silence. It wasn't an uncomfortable vacuum. Rather, it was more like catching our collective breath after weeks of endless conversation. A mutual sigh of relief. Out of nowhere I quipped, "We would have made beautiful children." She replied without skipping a beat "with our luck we would have had dark, giant Amazon girls and pale, fine-boned squirts of boys". We both laughed. She added, "Though trying would have been fun." She had fired the first salvo, and it was a direct hit. She had stopped me in my tracks, and she knew it. Let the games begin, I thought to myself.

We entered the restaurant and attracted immediate attention. I was used to it because of my height. She seemed unaffected. I may have misled you by saying that there was nothing outrageous about her. The truth was; she was flawless. Beautiful would be the general consensus of both men and women. Most importantly, she was beautiful by my unique definition. She had mastered the everyday, and was able to devote considerable attention to the smallest of details. She never walked without taking my arm in such a graceful manner, that it made you feel she had become an extension of you. When I helped her with her chair, she reached up and back with an expertly manicured hand; clasped my wrist. and whispered "thank you".

The restaurant was in the rear of the building. It was a bright airy space with a high wood and glass ceiling, tall windows and cobblestone floors. The small tables were arranged with many large plants and linen partitions. This combination maintained a good view of the room and the surrounding gardens, while providing a sense of intimacy. The piano bar from which we had entered accomplished the same feat with dark woods, minimal lighting and comfortable leather chairs.

As we were handed our menus, I noticed that the waning sunlight had lost the battle to the inconspicuous, but well placed spotlights, making the extensive menu featuring wood fired grill specialties legible. While reading our menus, the waiter lit our candles that were enclosed in a rustic brass and glass holder. I looked up from my menu as Marcel asked me if I had discovered anything interesting. What I saw lit the fuse on what was to be a delightful and memorable evening.

The warm glow of candlelight accented the natural contours of her delicately featured face. She had obviously planned her makeup for candlelight because the change in light had totally transformed her look. When I saw her, my amazement must have shown. Upon seeing my face Marcel calmly and coyly said, "I'm not on the menu, at least not until dessert". The smile she gave me as she returned her glance to the menu would have made Lucifer himself proud.

I had regained my composure by the time the waiter returned to take our order. She surprised me by closing her menu and saying "pick something for me; not too light, but not too heavy." Her eyes were fixed on me, as I responded immediately, "the lady will have your specialty, the herb crusted stuffed chicken breast, new potatoes and salad with the house vinaigrette and a glass of Chardonnay. I ordered Veal Marsala, new potatoes and a salad with Russian dressing, and a glass of Riesling. I explained to her after the waiter had left that the chicken was twice cooked. Baked then finished over the wood fire. It made for an incredible combination of flavors. She looked at me over tented hands and said, "Perfect"

"Let's talk," she said, as I felt my left calf being massaged between two silky feet. Her expression never changed; mine most certainly did.

We toasted the purity of our blossoming relationship with water, and the flirting began in earnest. We barely noticed when the food arrived; our conversation didn't miss a beat. She complimented me on my choice; I asked her whether she meant the meal, or the company. The piano music that drifted into the restaurant from the bar was now the background to her laughter. Our conversation was evidently interesting to a couple dining across the aisle. We caught them on more than one occasion obviously listening in, no longer talking to each other. The waiter didn't seem to mind the amount of time we spent, as he was enjoying watching us feeding each other dessert. We ordered two selections, and as advertised Marcel was on the menu. She stuck her finger in each one alternately and fed them to me to help me "decide which one I wanted". When I hesitated, she said, "Try this." She repeated the process with her fingers, this time smearing one dessert on her top lip, and the other on the bottom. As I took each lip between both of mine in turn, holding each just a few, but truly wonderful seconds, I heard both her and seemingly the entire room sigh.

We ordered coffee and Marcel announced that she had to visit the "ladies". As I rose from the table, I was buffeted by the swirling breeze generated by the rapid turning of all the male heads in the room. Marcel rose without taking her eyes from me. She dabbed at something at the corner of my mouth with her napkin as she went by, purposely brushing against me. She walked away from me… I was in a trance, along with all the rest of the sighted population in the room. She reached the wall and instead of just turning left she stopped, looking slowly, confidently back over her left shoulder. Her glance was daring, challenging. It seemed to be saying. How dare you? Looking at me that way, thinking those thoughts that you're thinking! Yet at the same time; she fully expected, no demanded that I look at her that way! The woman at the next table who had been taking in the whole evening finally had had enough. She slapped her husband and shrilled, "Why don't you look at me like that anymore?" and left the table in a huff. It was the only sour note in an otherwise perfect symphony of an evening.

I escorted her to my car, let her in and walked around to get in the driver's side clearing my head in the cool autumn night on the way. The interior light revealed that Marcel had slightly turned toward the center console awaiting my return. I started the car to add heat that our evening really didn't need. As I reached for the console to put the car in gear, Marcel raised the hem of her dress approximately three inches. She both revealed and offered me the width of my hand of her left thigh. She had remembered one of our conversations. I had told her of my "fetish". The feel of women's legs in stockings comforted me. It was an intimacy thing; my thing. Those who understood it, enjoyed it too. If I were comfortable with you, enamored with you, then I would massage your legs. For the first time, she looked apprehensive. I turned and while looking directly in her eyes; I called her three inch offer on her right side then raised her another four inches, squeezing both thighs as I went. I turned back to put the car in gear and returned my hand to her now fully exposed thighs. I heard her whisper "perfect" in the darkness.

It was early by Saturday night standards, around 11:30. I had a couple of options of where to take Marcel next, but nothing definite. After a few minutes of mutually enjoyable "massaging" on the freeway, a much more relaxed version of the alto refrain that I had grown so fond of said, "It's a long way back to my house." "I hope you have some sort of "collection" at your house, that you've been dying to show me." I could "hear" her sly smile in darkness.

Upon reaching my home, I led her straight to the family room. I put some unnecessary mood music on and returned to the sofa where Marcel had already removed the only thing that she would take off that evening. I stepped over the neatly placed suede pumps; looked into her eyes, and she literally leaped into my arms. We made out like teenagers on the sofa. Twice falling clumsily off of it, stopping to laugh and pant, trying to catch our collective breath. Our passion was intense, the result of weeks of telephone "foreplay". After several quivers, a few quakes and a couple of massive explosions, I could confidently put Marcel's name alongside that of St. Helen's, Etna, and Vesuvius; although we didn't actually physically consummate the relationship. "Let's go to sleep" she weakly suggested. I took her hand and led her upstairs to my bedroom. I left her standing in the middle of the floor, as I selected my favorite T-shirt from a drawer. I went into the master bath and put out her towels and toiletries. She was exhausted, but she smiled her approval. I led her into the bathroom; closed the door behind her and quickly undressed and put on light weight sweat pants that coordinated with the T-shirt. I had almost dozed off by the time she emerged from the bathroom and slid into bed with me. She squirmed until she reached the perfect "spooning position" then looked back over her shoulder to insure that she had achieved the intended effect. She drowsily said, "Good Night" and went immediately to sleep. I held her now limp, feather-light body in my arms and admired her beauty. I quickly replayed the evening in my head to jump-start my dreams, and fell into a deep sleep.

We awoke simultaneously, as the sun shone brightly between the windblown drapes. Today however, the sun played second fiddle to Marcel's smile. "Good Morning," she cheerfully said. "Let's make breakfast together." I smiled and got up to shower, though deep down I wanted to stay in bed with her. "Wow, maybe I shouldn't have played it coy last night," she said, as I undressed in front of her. "Your loss honey, I retorted", as I walked toward the bathroom door. "A girl can always change her mind," she said in a voice that stopped me in my tracks. I turned back to find that the "look" she had was just as devastating in the daylight. Many a great night have been destroyed by daylight, but not this one!

We worked well together in the kitchen and produced a feast of our favorite dishes. We lingered over brunch for almost two hours. I was served a final cup of coffee and Marcel dashed upstairs to change clothes. My T-shirt had been transformed into a work of art by her mannequin perfect legs. She returned, having deftly dressed down last night's outfit for the daytime. It was my first glance at her "normal" shade of lipstick, but that's a story for another day. We rode back to her car in relative silence, holding hands all the way. A simple kiss and a promise to see each other soon, and I was returning home on the wings of her voice; propelled by her smile.

Upon entering the house, I was glad that I could still smell her. It was a brand new house and I hadn't noticed how sterile it had been until now, just like my life. I went to my room and found the bed made. Smiling. I couldn't resist the urge to lie where Marcel had lain. Cradling her pillow as if it were she, I recalled her softness and refreshed my senses. Suddenly, feeling a bit self-conscious, I rolled over onto my pillow to find a small pair of black nylon gauze-like panties. A pleasant and not so subtle reminder that yes, Marcel was here!

# Chapter Twenty-Nine

## Metallic Mulberry
### And other permanently indelible impressions

She entered my life like a summer breeze. She was one part beauty, one part grace. She was spiced by equal measures of wisdom, strength and warmth. The sum of her caused me to shiver. Never before had a woman simultaneously stimulated all facets of my being.

Her presence is a study of contradiction. She was a fragile beauty with a rock solid conviction. "Barely black" appearance and a bottomless soul. Her steel-trap mind was softened by whimsical laughter. Eyes that melt you; cause you to float on air. Yet with a flash, she can send you back to your corner with a laser like stare.

All this confusion you might think would befuddle. But the fact is I grew in the glow of her aura, like a dormant seed in the cold dark desert of lost hope. Then nourished by the warmth of her smile, moisture of her kiss and light of her eyes my creativity budded and bloomed again; only to be killed by her need to be "free".

Have I been permanently affected by this brief encounter? Has my house now a home; been freshened by your aroma, like no spring airing can accomplish? Have not the hues and textures been enriched by the simple fact that "Marcel" was here. Absolutely!

The thing that I must tell you "Marcel" is that while you were with me you transformed that dormant seed into the bulb of my favorite flower, the tulip. The embodiment of eternal hope. In that bulb is stored the energy to bloom again. The energy of love, yes love "Marcel". No, I may not know you that well, but to know you at all is to love you. My final hope is that in your need to be free; there is also a need to be near me, at least to call. I know you hear the "music" Marcel. I just hope it will someday lead you home to me

Submitted with passionate, respectful, and undying love

Jim

Thirty

Beautiful

I have described my experiences with a number of wonderful women. All were memorable for various reasons. Not all of my memories of them were favorable, but they shared a common thread. They were all beautiful women. Now before you judge me as shallow and superficial. I should probably explain my definition of beautiful.

Have you ever noticed that your ex-lovers are never as attractive to you after your relationship as ended? No matter how the relationship ended they just don't look the same to you afterward. That's because the eyes of love play tricks on you. You become blind to the cosmetic flaws, and of course the character faults that are apparent to everybody else. After the love is gone you see the same person and think. What did I see in him or her?! That kind of attraction was mainly physical, not that there is anything wrong with that. I admit that there is a major dose of physical passion in my relationships, but I maintain that my attractions are based on a much deeper principal and more individual set of preferences. It is what I call beautiful.

The people who think they know me. (You know who you are.) The ones that try to define who I am by their own standards don't really understand. They say that I have a physical "type" that they can define. While it is true that there are certain physical attributes that attract me. They are not the usual ones that may first come to mind. The types of characteristics that I'm talking about are subtle, personal and very subjective. The kinds of things that do not age, sag, or turn gray. They are timeless, boundless and affect all of the senses. They are the stuff that keeps you awake at night, after the relationship ends. You wonder if someone else is enjoying that special something that you miss so much. Many of the traits are an integral part of the nicknames that I gave to the ladies.

Beautiful is not necessarily a physical state, although your mind interprets it as attractiveness. It is an emotional awareness, a heightened sense of self and the effect you have on your surroundings. It is effortless and probably transparent to those that have it, but devastatingly apparent to others, even other women. It is not sex appeal per se, although the traits arouse sexual receptors. It cannot be faked, copied or ignored. They excite men and sometimes infuriate women. But because of the random nature of their effect, some men may be totally oblivious to the same thing that drives another man wild.

It is a smile, a turn of the head, a stance. The way a look of surprise, wonder or a knowing glance can change, enhance or make the most common event special in your mind. The casual way she may handle a compliment or an off-handed remark. One of my personal favorites is the lilt in the voice. That combined with wit and the art of conversation (a dying art I might add) is a combination that is almost impossible to resist. I will illustrate my point with a comparison of cars. Any car is capable of taking you from point A to point B safely, economically and in reasonable comfort. But take that same trip in a Mercedes, and you'll get a totally different and very memorable experience. You don't even mind the additional expense.

If you don't believe this principle exists; take notice in your workplace how men never mind doing favors for certain women, but not others. Which women get flowers or invited out to expensive restaurants on their first dates instead of the local chain bistro. Some women get more consideration with a five-minute conversation and a smile, than others can accomplish with six months of butt-naked sex. Make no mistake, beautiful is a very powerful emotional tool.

Beautiful is borne from intelligence; nurtured by grace, enhanced by heavy doses of confidence, sensitivity and compassion. The fact that is so very important to understand is that the trait that I call beautiful is about how the women takes the time and effort to make you feel better about yourself for having experienced her. The woman does make the dress!

# Chapter Thirty-One

## Pet Names

I have taken great care to maintain the anonymity of my former partners. I will continue this trend by using their pet names when describing their attributes.

Sizzle – Small, coal black eyes housed in a classically structured face that belied the hidden passion. She possessed a tremendous sense of style.

Cayenne – Bright-eyed and large-mouthed seemingly filled with at least forty teeth, always arranged in a smile.

Music – Polish, grace and fashion were just a couple of her many talents. She was a tremendous conversationalist with a voice that you could listen to forever.

Carbon – Creative, high-spirited and possibly the kindest woman I've ever met. She possesses what I like to call the "eyes of wonder".

Silk – Probably the most versatile woman I have ever met. She was athletic yet graceful.  Her spirit was passionate and aggressive. She possessed the most graceful lines and softest skin humanly possible.

Porcelain – Strong, hard working and intelligent. She was exotic, warm and passionate with a great sense of humor.

Kryptonite – Probably the most sensual and naturally sexy woman I've ever encountered.

Chapter Thirty-Two

Marcel

The Day the Music Died

The title of the story seems to give away the ending, but nothing could be further from the truth. Actually this portion of the story is more about the journey than the destination. One could not help but ask how did a relationship that seemed to have so much promise end up crashing on the rocks the way it did? What did one or both of us do wrong? Who was the villain? When did the relationship seem to take a wrong turn? Where does it stand today, if at all?

The answers to all of these questions are contained in the next few pages and come dangerously close to discussing the "Why" question. These emotions will be all too familiar to those who have had their hearts broken. Unfortunately, the "truths" about love will be just as mysterious after reading this as before. At least you'll know that it has happened to someone other than you.

The holiday season can be tough on any relationship. Ours was no exception. You want to be with that special someone. Alas, we both had families with fairly young children, jobs, ex-spouses etc. We survived it with maturity; understanding, phone calls and a glorious shopping trip. We met on Christmas Eve for lunch and finalized our plans. We were going to shop until it was time for Marcel to pick up her son and go to the airport. She had to take him back to the East Coast to be with his father's family for Christmas. For those of you that have never been in the North at Christmas time; well you don't know what you are missing. I've been in Florida and Arizona in December and it's just not the same. We walked in the New England Style downtown of my home city. It consists of rows of locally owned small shops connected to a new pedestrian "lifestyle" shopping complex. All of the storefronts were elaborately decorated. The sound of bells filled the air, from sleigh bells attached to the doors of the stores, to the Salvation Army hand bell. In the background, the church tower bells were playing Christmas carols. There was the aroma of a street vendor selling roasted nuts, mixing with the smell of pine, both real and artificial. In this upscale community, on this special day, everyone had a shopping bag and a smile.

It had long been my practice to reserve one purchase for Christmas Eve, just to be involved in the last minute atmosphere. It was probably a holdover from my days of having young children. Anyway, the purchase having been made at the sporting goods store; I was free to concentrate on the serious business of window shopping with Marcel. We held hands as we strolled in a large circle, stopping at every expertly decorated window. She looked great wearing a black and white wool hounds tooth mini-skirt, black tights, demi-boots, and a black two piece angora sweater set. The ensemble was topped by a leather car length, shawl collared jacket, a medium lavender hat and scarf, and black calfskin gloves. I thought they were the softest thing I had ever felt until she turned to me, removed one glove, took my hand, and gave me that patented look with the raised eyebrow, and said "I want to really feel your touch before I go". The beret and scarf matched her lipstick almost perfectly and together beautifully accented the contours of her now rosy complexion. A light snow began to fall, as we kissed under a sprig of mistletoe suspended from a storefront. The warmth of our embrace melted the fine snow as it landed in our faces, and added a new dimension to the tingling sensation, causing both of us to laugh.

We turned and continued our walk with only one more store to see before we reached the parking lot and Marcel's departure. It was the jewelry store. As we walked, I explained that this was the store where I had purchased the cufflinks that she loved. It was also where I had designed and ordered my kids' custom sports and music jewelry. They cherished the pieces that I had given them, both as a keepsake and remembrance of how proud I was of their hard work and dedication. The jewelry store window had a dazzling display of Waterford crystal, Sterling silver serving trays, bone china and rings. Men's rings, cocktail rings and of course engagement rings. We made comments and our personal preferences known;

just as we had done for every other window display. Then with sad hearts and leaden feet we walked to the parking lot. I watched her drive away after a warm embrace and a quick goodbye. She had a son to pickup and a plane to catch.

Marcel called me on New Year's Eve at eleven as we had planned. We talked until after midnight, ending with our first "virtual encounter" of the year. A "vivid" discussion of what was going to happen when we saw each other at the end of the month.

We both had a brutal travel schedule planned for January, so it didn't seem unusual to talk to Marcel less than I normally did. I called her after a particularly good day on the road to see how she was fairing. She picked up the phone and burst into tears. "I've been confused lately", she confessed. "I've missed you, but I have also been dreading talking to you" she continued. I sat quietly, confused yet knowing. I put on my metaphorical blindfold and waited for the command of "Fire". She explained through genuinely painful tears, that I had taken her completely by surprise. She had married young, had children young and now that she was free; she wanted to stay that way. She didn't want to abuse my love for her, as many had in the past. She knew what my goal in life was, and that I wasn't going to accept the role of "suitor in waiting". I could no longer distinguish the words. I was numb. I had heard words similar to these in the past and now I was just immune to them. I must be the most loved yet rejected man alive; I thought. Why does every woman I fall in love with want more than anything to get away from me? Oops! There goes the "why" question. Marcel said "the fact that she didn't run screaming from the jewelry store let her know that she was in dangerous territory and to save me greater pain in the future, she thought it better to end it now".

The silence on the phone echoed the sudden vacuum in my midsection. There was no heartache, no wrenching in the intestines, no immediate need to vomit. It was a surgical strike. She closed the wound by saying "I love you, but I would only hurt you". I sat there holding the phone in shock long after she had hung up. I stood up after the anesthetic of her voice had worn off. I wasn't angry, but I was instantly lonely. As time wore on however, I respected the honesty of her words and the conviction of her position. I didn't try to measure how much she missed me, if at all. I didn't torture myself questioning what she was doing or with who? I just worked, harder than I had ever worked before.

It was a glorious day in June. I had just completed my last tax return of the season. The grind was over. I celebrated by taking a stroll on the grounds after returning from the Post Office. I went to my office to put away the last of the files and noticed that I had received a call while I was out. Dreading a last minute request, I sat and listened to the message. "Hi Jim, this is Marcel". The voice was as recognizable as an old Motown hit, and just as soothing. It took me back instantly. "I just called to see how your campaign turned out. I really miss you. But please don't try to call me, not yet". I took the message to mean that she really did love me and I was energized. I didn't believe that she was coming back, but at least I didn't feel that I had been in love alone. You may call me foolish, but you didn't hear the voice.

I didn't actually see her until November of that year. She called saying that "she would love to see me, if I wasn't angry with her." I gave her directions to my new residence. She arrived looking tired from her quest for the future, having slogged through the present, running from her past. She had good news of a new job that was starting in two weeks in Texas, but there was no joy in her face. She needed a place to stay until that time. I offered her my hospitality, but she quickly refused. "I don't want to take advantage of you", she said. "I told her that she was always welcome in my home." She agreed to stay in one of the extra bedrooms. At about 2 am, she quietly slipped into my room and under the sheets, squirming to get comfortable in the "spooning" position. When she settled, I said "perfect" and she fell immediately to sleep.

She spent four days with me. We passed the time reading, taking walks and talking about how I was going to decorate the house. We cooked for each other, sampled wines and drank hot chocolate by the fire in the evenings. On the third day, I showed her all of the places she could find keys outside of the house, and told her that she was always welcome, even when I was on the road. She looked better by the day; the rest was doing her good. In many ways, she was treating me better than any girlfriend had ever done. She helped with chores around the house, and always made certain that I was comfortable. We ate all of our meals together and slept together each evening. We were friendly and intimate, but not lovers.

On the evening of the fourth day, she addressed the white elephant in the room that we had both been ignoring for different reasons. We were sharing our second glass of wine in the fire lit family room. Marcel began to speak without looking at me. "You know you are going to have to move on". I answered her in a monotone voice, "I know".

The house seemed incredibly empty upon my return from taking Marcel to the airport. I did some chores to keep busy. I smiled as I saw the laundry that Marcel had done before she left. As I put away the linens and came to my underwear, I discovered the perfumed lace trimmed white satin panties Marcel had left me. The tradition continued. Marcel had been here. But when, if ever would she return?

Our relationship evolved and grew even though we spoke on the phone just periodically and e-mailed each other only occasionally. We laughed about the good times, cried about the bad, and gave each other career and parenting advice. She traveled extensively and was a social butterfly. She told me about the events she attended. Always listing the people she had met and detailing the outfits she wore, paying special, though subtle attention to her undergarments, maintaining the "tradition". In one memorable discussion she calmly stated, "There was no way I could wear anything under that dress; the way the material clung". I could "hear the look". She always gave me something to hold on to. She was the only ex-girlfriend that I corresponded with. The reason was simple, respect. I respected her as a woman, her integrity, and genuine interest in my issues. But most important was her respect for my feelings. Unlike any other woman I had been involved with; I could count on Marcel.

This fact was again proven when I told her about a huge dinner meeting I had scheduled with some investors in a new business venture that I was starting. It was the kind of function that required a spouse or special significant other. Without prompting, she enthusiastically said. "When do you need me there?" Marcel was perfect for the role. She quizzed me on the type of women the "wives" were and details about the business venture. Then she asked me about wardrobe. I said nostalgically, I'll wear my "first date suit". She said "perfect", it fit the occasion, but we disagreed on whether I should wear a pocket square to give the suit a little flair. I always preferred to err on the side of conservatism. We agreed to disagree.

On the night of the function, Marcel met me at the restaurant, which was near the airport. She had come to town from Florida specifically for the occasion. She emerged from the restroom looking like a goddess in burgundy, matching my tie and sporting a sophisticated hairdo. She approached me without saying a word, opened her small clutch purse and removed a delicate pair of burgundy satin panties. I knew this because as she re-folded them in front of me, I detected the heavenly blended scent of beautiful woman and expensive perfume. She expertly arranged them in my jacket pocket without removing her eyes from mine. Then with raised eyebrow she said, "Now the investors will be irresistibly drawn to you and won't know why." She gave me a pat on the butt and took my arm the way only she could and said, "Now let's go make some money."

Marcel continued to visit me whenever she was in town, until I finally started a new relationship. Her advice; be careful, be happy. We continue to be friends to this day even though we've not seen each other in years. She has re-married and is very happy. I was invited to the wedding, but my heart wouldn't allow my body to attend. I was surprised how much it still hurt to think she was getting married. I am positive that she understood my position, because her final act as a single woman was to text me a description of her panties, ten minutes before she was scheduled to walk down the aisle. "Perfect". I will always love her.

# Autopsy of a Romantic

He seemed too young to be there, undeserving of his fate.

His battered and bruised body was in stark contrast with the calm of his face.

His death presented a problem, a mystery to be solved.

What was it that brought this man prematurely to this place?

His scalp was grayer than it should be, from excess worry no doubt.

His brown eyes once filled with warmth, possessing sight so keen.

Were now glazed over, retinas scorched by the indiscretions he had seen.

His ears had been finely tuned so that beauty could be heard.

Now he lay there with eardrums numbed by lies; painful and absurd.

From his throat, eroded by years of acid churning; had come a voice that was inspiring and reassuring.

His fresh healthy lungs had provided plenty of air.

He bore the weight and unhappiness of carrying relationships far beyond repair.

His broad shoulders and arms were muscular, still strong.

Made so by his habit of holding on too long.

His hands were worn smooth, the remnants of old wounds strewn about.

They were most likely the result of him tirelessly lending them out.

His fully developed spinal cord gave him abundant feelings to share.

But it left him painfully susceptible to those who did not care.

His digestive system supplied him with energy to burn.

Sadly, it couldn't provide the lesson his brain refused to learn.

His lower torso probably caused him more than its share of grief, the joints showing signs of great strain

But he obviously didn't die of that kind of pain.

There was only part of him that had given more that it had to give.

It had been deprived of the nourishment that it needed to live.

His body was larger; stronger than most.

A gift he gladly used to serve.

He was born with the capacity to accomplish great things.

He gave more than they deserved.

The answer to the mystery of why this man had died was written carefully on a card and to his toe was tied.

The examiner methodically sewed together a body; that once again had been torn apart.

As he pulled the sheet to cover him, the examiner sadly sighed and mumbled as he completed his report.

"Before me lies an otherwise healthy man. Cause of death, a broken heart"


James R. Russell

# Chapter Thirty-Four

## Letters

## Silk

Dear Silk:

In reply to your calls, I am well. I have been busy. It is my most hectic time of the year in the tax business. Additionally, one of my new businesses has been launched. The other two companies that are scheduled to begin operations this year are on track. I am also trying to put the finishing touches on my house deal. With any "luck" I will take possession as early as this weekend. I say luck, but I really mean that if it is to be; it will be.

This is not to say that I have been too busy to call. On the contrary, I have chosen not to call you. Only I can determine what the rest of my life will be about, what's important to me. A "life partner" should believe in the same things or at a minimum respect the differences. I can only surmise that based on the way situations have been handled, that there is just no future in this for me. My future hopefully includes a person that I can always count on. Not for the best in the world, that would be unrealistic. No one is perfect. No, I don't want perfection, but I do expect and deserve a loving, committed, honest and respectful consistency. I seek a fertile environment of love, peace and harmony where both "life partners" can grow and prosper. What you may not realize is that the things that I required, although different than some of your needs are just as important to me as yours are to you.

Well, I have decided to just give up. I can't change the way you are any more than I can alter who I am. Why should either of us change? I just wanted time, commitment; affection and respect from someone that professes to love me. That, in my opinion is not too much to ask. But it is something upon which I cannot compromise. In the final analysis, you have shown me that you are not willing or able to provide what I need and deserve. I can no longer pretend that you are remorseful about you actions, or the way they make me feel. Especially considering there is no real mention of the offense to me or any attempt on your part to somehow correct it. It is not so much the actions themselves individually, it's the fact that they've continued to happen. I have always conducted myself such that you could feel comfortable in coming to me about anything. I have always said that people seldom regret the things they do; only the things they don't do. That is what this is about. It is why I am so incredibly sad and sorry about the whole situation. The fact that neither you nor I will be able to benefit from the blessings that love would undoubtedly provide us.

I don't regret for a moment loving you despite the outcome, because I was able to do something that made me extremely happy. That is, to love a woman that I think is the most wonderful person I have ever encountered. On the other hand, people don't get into relationships just to love someone. They also need to be loved in return.

When you love someone, you just make a way to do things for them. The human spirit allows for that, if it is important to you. It has been painfully illustrated that I am not nearly as important to you as I should be. When you love someone you don't continue to ask them to accept something that to him is unacceptable. When I saw you last you promised to do three things. Having you do those things was very important to me. You did none of them in the manner you stated. As a former athlete, you know that in order to make the game winning shot, you have to do it before the buzzer. Otherwise, it is just show and doesn't count. Special acts; gifts and favors are in addition to, not in lieu of the basics. I cannot assign myself to a life of battling and begging for, and ultimately living with the disappointment of not receiving the things that should flow from you naturally. It is time for me to take some of my own reportedly good advice. You have shown me "where you want to live". I have to accept the fact that even if I wanted to live "there" you have not made a place for me in your life. I have to walk in another direction, because I keep falling in that same "hole". It is the fault of no one, but in order to avoid the inevitable fall and resulting pain, I have to do something else.

You will always remain alive in my heart and my mind's eye; forever young, beautiful; delightful and intelligent. It is tremendously regrettable to me, that such a person will not be a part of the rest of my life. I do this not because I no longer love you, or because of someone or something else. It is just the realization that if I can't trust you with the least of things, then surely it would not be prudent of me to put the rest of my life in your care.

In closing or final explanation of how I feel, I pose to you the following rhetorical question. Where would you have been, or be right now if I was as attentive to your needs, as responsible to my commitments and overall as intuitive or compassionate to your situations as you have been to me and mine?

I leave you with all my hopes and prayers for a bright and promising future; full of happiness, peace, success and love. Yes love, because I know the joy that true love can bring. I know that God has not let me experience the bliss of our love without someday bringing someone to provide that feeling forever. I also could not claim to love you as much as I do without wanting you to experience the same thing, even if it unfortunately is not being supplied by me. Please, when you are again blessed with the precious love of another human being, cherish it for all that it is worth. To do that you must return it; and it will always multiply in its benefit to you. This I know to be true. Goodbye my love. Your effect on me will be everlasting.

All my Love forever

Jim

Chapter Thirty-Five

KRYPTON

An indescribable mystic experience

I first gazed upon her one fine October day. A day filled with darkness and despair until she happened my way. I sensed that my luck had changed, but I could never have imagined how much until I saw her angelic face. Krypton is a colorless; odorless gas, but yet I detected her scent. I was compelled to follow. I knew not where I went. I knew that I had to know her, but that meant taking a chance of monumental proportions.

I entered the room and spoke to her. The sight of her aura was blinding. The room was filled with Krypton. I felt as though I couldn't breathe, my heart was in the ceiling. Just when I thought I could stand no more she looked at me and spoke. I cannot remember what she said, for my mind had gone blank. Her eyes so warm and deep; she had seemed to sense my pain, notice my fear and were putting those thoughts to sleep. As her magical powers increased I began to relax. The healing light of her aura combined with the lighter than air properties of the gas replaced my sorrow with every breath I took.

When I left the room that day, my life was forever changed. I began to hope for better things. Upon our second meeting, I knew what I had dreamt was real. This beautiful creature would positively alter the rest of my scheduled life. Her eyes were again soothing but my focus was changed. Now it was her smile that captivated me. Her words were mesmerizing. My attention was divided by those teeth, until I recognized that I had lost my emotional balance. I felt myself falling totally out of control. She stroked her hair, beautiful soft strands that seemed to stretch out like a safety net securing my floating heart. After lunch I sat totally drained, exhausted from the exchange of energy. I realized that krypton, like many other gases, had many other forms. She kissed me goodbye and my spirits soared. I was revived by the lighter than air vapor that sent my soul on a thrill ride that to date no roller coaster had matched. But what goes up must come down according to the laws of science. Like a gust of wind, dispersing the gas, she was gone.

The solid form of krypton had appeared in all its mighty glory. In a split second, she had become all business. After careful analysis, I realized that this was the thing I loved most about her. She was as brilliant as she was beautiful. Our short relationship was intense; white hot passion, intellectual stimulation, the ultimate blend of overt sexuality and genius. The combination of her powers and the seamless way she flowed between them, kept me on an emotional rocking horse.

Unfortunately, she used her powers for evil. The relationship was marred by lies and deception. Finally, my rational side took over. After analyzing the emotional "T" account, the pain outweighed the pleasure. When I confronted her, she called me her Superman. I countered that regrettably she was Kryptonite to me, and I had to leave her to survive. I still can hear her siren like voice as she called out after me "I'll miss you".

# Chapter Thirty-Six

## Rhonda

The depth of my depression had reached an all-time low point. Not even the rigorous pace of the recently concluded tax campaign had been able to snap me from my zombie-like malaise. In past instances, my dedication to the work allowed me to compartmentalize my sadness and push on. This time I was forced to hire additional temporary staff to compensate for my lack of interest, energy and focus. The lull in my professional life forced me to realize that something had to be done. Admittedly, I had a full plate. I had full custody of my kids with their busy schedules, while my ex-wife convalesced after a lengthy medical battle, managing a growing tax practice, coaching two baseball teams that had just finished their summer season, with football coming up in a month. I needed a break. The problem had to be fixed. It took too much energy to mask the symptoms.

I decided to go on vacation; to the place where I knew that I could recharge my batteries, refresh my spirit, and most importantly forget. It is my hope that everyone has the opportunity to travel and hopefully find that one place where their spirit is at rest. A place where they can truly enjoy the beauty of nature and revel in its healing power. That place for me is Arizona. Although I enjoy the beach, mountains and woods; the desert is my special place. Its sheer size minimizes any and all problems that may be troubling you. There are spots where you can see more than one-hundred miles in every direction without seeing a single living thing. However, alone is never lonely; there is always the wind, cacti, sun and shadow. The mere fact that life can survive the incredibly harsh conditions combined with the beauty, complexity and grandeur of the rock formations comfort you with the assurance of the presence of a higher power.

It was the fourth day of seven that I would be based in Phoenix. I had taken a series of day trips, seen the local sights, bought myself some presents and enjoyed nightlife. I had planned an aggressive schedule for the day; driving north in the eastern third of the state to see the Petrified Forest, Crater Lake, and Monument Valley, Utah then west to Flagstaff and finally South to Sedona by mid to late afternoon, so that I could still make it back to Phoenix in time to take in a baseball game in their new stadium.

At five am I departed, fueled by buckwheat pancakes, coffee and excitement. I drove northward, as the sun rose over the dusty peaks of the Camelback Mts. It was the first of many amazing sights I would see that day. My schedule was almost perfect, I didn't see the crater, but I spent special moments in the Petrified Forest and saw three rainbows simultaneously in Monument Valley. I wish I was a better photographer. After a memorable visit to a train museum in Flagstaff and a great lunch; I headed for Sedona.

Sedona, AZ is a small tourist town about ninety miles northwest of Phoenix on Highway 89A. It unofficially marks the beginning of the Red Rock Country from the South and 89A rises quickly into the conifer forests of the higher elevations. The scenery is breathtaking. I can't describe it. It has to been seen to be believed. Everything in the area bows in deference to the landscape. Even the local outlet of a world-wide fast food chain is not exempt. Its arches are not the customary golden color. They are teal so as to blend more naturally into the surroundings. Sedona's real claim to fame however, is its position as the center of cosmic energy, mysticism and the study and practice of alternative religions and beliefs.

I drove into town at about two-thirty, just as I had planned. I thought I would do some window shopping, get some ice cream and stretch my legs. I should have been happier than I was, with the day that I was having. Unfortunately, being the kind of person that always "thinks in terms of two" I was missing something. I began to think about Silk. I was no longer sure that I missed her, as much as I missed the bond that we had. It had been long enough since our break-up for me to be over her, but there was still a gaping hole in my soul where she used to live.

Walking aimlessly down the main commercial street, I found nothing that attracted my attention until I saw a sign advertising horse hair pottery. Authentic horse hair pottery is rare and fairly expensive. I needed a piece for my collection. Entering the small, crowded shop I noticed a locked display case with some impressive examples of this Native American artistry. Walking to the front of the store to get the attention of the sales clerk, I absently walked right into a woman who was in the middle of a transaction. I was mortified. She was a woman of shorter stature, about 5'2" with dark brown hair that she wore up in large loosely cabled braids. She wore a flowered loosely fitting garment. I made a clumsy apology, which got no response from her. Then I realized that I hadn't backed away from her! I was more nervous than ever. I looked at the sales clerk who gave me no help; but indicated that he would assist me as soon as he completed the transaction. I made another weak attempt at an apology. It was then that she finally turned, and while smiling said "It's alright. I understand." I felt the warmth of her smile through the 100 degree heat. She stood looking me up and down, her expression never changing. I backed away from her, almost knocking over a small display.

My mind was racing, I really wanted to talk to her, but what should I say? If I waited to buy a piece of pottery from the case, she would be gone forever. I could walk around the store pretending to shop, waiting for her to leave and talk to her on the way out. My current emotional state made me shy, indecisive. I picked up a small tourist size piece of pottery and headed apprehensively toward the counter. I stood a couple of feet behind her; just in range of her floral aroma. She wore a powder that sparkled on her shoulders, which contributed to the glow that emanated from her. I needed to talk to her, not in a sexual way, it was hard to describe. The clerk, who could see her face, was urging me to say something, but I stood dumbfounded as she gathered her belongings, and left the store without looking back. After a minute of talking to the clerk about the collection, I purchased the now meaningless piece of pottery and dejectedly left the store.

I was walking across the sidewalk toward an ice cream shop on the other side of the street; when suddenly out of nowhere she appeared saying, "It's about time, I thought you'd never come out". She smiled, took my arm and said "you look like you could use some ice cream" as we walked she said "my name is Rhonda, your spirit spoke to me". I began to say "my name is" she interrupted "they have great butter pecan ice cream at this shop, I had some yesterday". I stopped in my tracks. I said, "Butter pecan is the" she interrupted "I know, I had a dream about you!" I was amazed at how calm she was. She spoke to me as though she had known me for years. After buying me ice cream, she continued. "I'm a therapist. I live in a small town in the Northeast. Do you believe in the power of crystals?" Without waiting for an answer, she motioned to the entrance of a touristy gift shop. Pointing to a counter at the rear of the store she said "pick a crystal, whichever one you like". I chose a large red one; it looked like a garnet, my sister's birthstone Rhonda came to the counter paid the clerk, and asked directions to a local park. The clerk gave her directions and looked at me; "sure is a hot one today" he said. I asked if the monsoonal rains had started yet. "It hasn't rained in one hundred fifteen days" he said, wiping his brow as he looked at a marked calendar. Rhonda interrupted "finish your ice cream we have to go". As she exited the store Rhonda looked back and said to the clerk "it's going to rain today!" "Where's your car?" She said. I pointed up the street. Rhonda put the red crystal in my left hand and said "hold this tightly". She reached into a small pouch she carried and retrieved a small brown crystal which she put in her left hand and took my right hand as we walked to my car. As I drove she said "so how long has it been since she left you". I answered without hesitation. "It's been nine months. Is it that obvious?" I'm sure I looked stunned. "I knew you were sad, but I wasn't sure why until you picked that crystal." She continued, "Don't worry; I'm not trying to pick you up. My spirit is drawn to women right now." We rode in silence, but my mind clattered as it sped through everything that was happening. I decided to just go with it.

We walked through the park; all scrub grass and stunted shrubs. It did have a magnificent view of a painted mesa in the distance. Rhonda's voice was almost hypnotic. She bombarded me with positive mantras and good advice. Somehow it didn't come across as lecturing. She told me it wasn't my fault. All I had done was to love someone; there was no crime in that.

Suddenly, there were more trees and it was markedly cooler. Then out of nowhere was the inspiration for the marriage proposal I

wrote later. A glade of trees hid a cool stream that was fed by a
spring. It seemed to appear magically from nowhere. We sat on
a big flat rock, dangling our feet in the water, as I told her about
my relationship with Silk. She actually listened! We still held the
crystals. Then suddenly she looked at the sky and said, "It's time to
go".

When we reached the car she surprised me by saying "kiss me
Jim," as she threw her arms around my waist. As our lips touched
it began to rain, well what passes for rain in the desert. If you stood
still for five minutes you'd barely get damp.

"Stop at the gift shop" she said. I watched her put her crystal away,
and I was amazed to see that it was now colorless. We entered the
gift shop and Rhonda put the red crystal on the counter. The clerk
laughed; circled the date on the calendar and said, "You were right,
it did rain" We exited the store with a disposable camera which
Rhonda used to take two pictures of me. She had me take two pictures of her. She then asked a stranger to take three photos of us together. Finally, she asked me how she could contact me. I gave her
one of my business cards. I realized at that moment that I hadn't
told her my name. I asked her if she wanted to eat, she refused;
saying that she had to get back to her hotel. She didn't want a ride
either. "Her work was done" she said.

As I drove back to Phoenix the thunderstorm intensified. I wanted
to rehash my afternoon with Rhonda in my mind, but I had to
concentrate on the road, as the lightening seemed to get closer
and closer. It was as if I was descending from Mt. Olympus after
receiving a blessing from on high and the gods were making sure
that I didn't even look back. The closer I got to Phoenix; the better
I felt. It wasn't until I was halfway through my dinner, that I realized that I had missed the baseball game.

A few weeks later I was celebrating my birthday with my children,
not yet feeling full strength, but certainly a lot better than I had
been before the vacation. I had to comfort my youngest son after I
opened the present he had given me. He assumed that the tears in
my eyes meant that I was disappointed with the jigsaw puzzle he
had given me. I explained to all of them that the Arizona landscape

on the box was the exact scene that I had seen in a very special park while I was on vacation. It was another reminder of the magical afternoon I had spent with Rhonda and re-enforcement of the special power she had.

I received an unusual letter a week later. It was postmarked in Atlanta, and was missing a return address. I opened the envelope and found copies of each of the three pictures of Rhonda and me, taken in Arizona. Her smile brought back the warmth of the Arizona sun. Just looking at the pictures dissolved the last of the gray clouds of sadness that still plagued me occasionally. I kept my favorite picture on my desk, and it wasn't until a week later that I discovered the message on the back of one of the other pictures. It said simply, "you will find love very soon". It was less than one month before I heard the "Music".

## I Miss You

I miss our late night talks.

I wish we had taken more long walks.

We opened our hearts, shared our dreams and goals.

I reminisce about the way you pampered me, by gently rubbing my soles.

I miss how you say my name, the way your mouth does move.

Your uplifting spirit and sunny disposition keeps me in my groove.

Your eyes so warm and understanding, a voice as light as air.

I miss standing at your door, not knowing what you'll wear.

I recall the sway of your hips and the click of your heels on the kitchen floor.

The taste of those luscious lips, make me long for more.

I miss the way you cut my food, how you can set the mood.

The way you smile and don't mind; when it's "screw Lisa" on a list of "things to do" you find.

The thing I miss most, of all the wonderful things you do.

At the end of the day, hearing your musical voice saying "I missssed yoouu!"


Love Always,


Jim

# A Lover's Prayer

O Lord, clear their weary eyes and touch a broken heart.

So that they may see that we should never be apart.

Help them comprehend a love that glorifies us both.

To this I will testify, and pledge my lifelong oath.

Grant us the peace and serenity that only devotion brings,

Timeless, boundless concepts represented by two tiny golden rings.

I do not ask that you fill the valleys or solve the problems in my life.

I pray that you'll grant your most precious gift, a friend, a partner, a loving wife.

James Russell

# Marriage Proposal

Like the miracle of cool flowing water springing from the desert, quenching parched soils and spurring growth with its very presence.

As the invisible breeze gently parts an overcast sky, revealing the healing warmth of the ever-present sun.

Her voice came to me over a random phone line; one among millions, a song from the heavens. You give me happiness, unbridled joy.

A feeling I've not had since I was a boy.

Your love removes all sadness, takes away the pain.

I now bask in sunshine, no more clouds and rain.

You take me to a better place, devoid of heartache and strife.

I will love you always, for I pledge you my life.

Please dear; make me the happiest man alive.

Will you be my wife?

# Chapter Forty

## Porcelain

She appeared in my life quite by chance, a voice from nowhere; a gift to my ears. It was as if she spoke a dead language. Seldom used words strung together telling her story, but only a specialist, someone who listened with their heart could hear them. Words like commitment, fidelity, devotion and trust rolled off her tongue with ease and yet in a matter of fact tone that I knew was her own. She wasn't trying to impress me; rather these words were chosen carefully to inform the listener of her singleness of purpose, the importance of her search.

Her intensity and passion intrigued me, but there was still something about her that puzzled me. She had a quality that haunted me, and was very difficult to analyze over the phone. She seemed to be interested, but yet her emotions were regulated, a calculated calm. She had fashioned a thin shell around her heart, not a barrier to love just a necessary crust. She had been hurt before that was certain, but she was definitely a lover of love. I realized that I must meet her in person to experience firsthand, the warmth I felt even over the phone. Maybe, I had found in her the soul mate I'd yearned for, my missing half. In her presence, I also hoped to find the answer to the mystery that eluded me over the phone.

When I first met her, I was more than pleasantly surprised. Her uncommon beauty momentarily stunned my senses. She was just as complex in person as over the phone. At first glance, she had beautiful black hair that shaded a sharp mind. Her incredible ginger brown eyes were mysterious and knowing, yet warm and inviting. She had shiny full lips; they made you think bad thoughts. Her smile was nervous but friendly, with teeth that drew you in. She oozed maturity, but her youthful body was built for sin. We traded tentative glances and investigative words. I sensed she was probing, trying to determine my worth. I knew I was interested, but I couldn't pinpoint why. I reached for her hand and felt her warmth. She made no advances, nor did she resist.

I didn't know it at the time, but each little kiss peeled away a piece of the protective crust that she had built. Every layer I removed exposed a bit more of her internal glow.

The first time she kissed me we were under a streetlight. When my tongue met hers, I knew it was right. When she held me I knew I was loved, like the feeling I first felt when I was still young. At that moment, deep down inside I wanted nothing more than to make her be mine. She reassured me when I touched her breasts and she squealed with joy. I worried a bit when she helped unzip my pants and said not a word, but gave her approval with eyes that said yum-yum and an eager mouth that screamed it's about time!!!

Who was this woman that had tied me in knots? Of what was she made? What was she about? Did I know any more about her than when I first spoke to her? Did it matter if I didn't? How could a woman be so soft and yet so tough? How could she contain so much substance and remain thin? Have such emotional grit and not be rough? More importantly, was I out of control and in trouble again?

The time spent with her solidified our bond; we discovered we were more alike than not. Still, I could not find that one trait that defined who she was, one material that embodied her essence, the thing that set her apart. Her name; the gift to her that defines her intangible love in a solid physical way, as seen through my loving eyes.

It came to me one day; the way many great ideas do, by accident. I was looking at her, admiring her sunlit profile. The sun simultaneously warmed her cheeks, brightened her smile, and added a glow to her eyes. Her visage was stunning. Then it hit me; the thing to which I was hypnotically and unconsciously drawn. She had looked the same way in the moonlight the previous night.

She had mastered the character trait that is so elusive in people, consistency. She had successfully layered the delicate, fragile and usually mutually exclusive physical attributes of beauty and sexiness, with intelligence and wit. That had been combined with love, devotion, compassion, integrity and spirituality. These individually thin nearly transparent attributes had been so expertly bonded as to make them appear as one. Each layer enhancing the previous, creating a solid, substantial yet exquisitely detailed form. She possessed timeless beauty and amazing strength all while remaining delicate and fragile.

She is complete and wonderful, needing neither modification nor alteration. Showing my love for her is simply to put her in the bright light that she so richly deserves. To appreciate the creation that she already is, to cherish her place in my life and remind her how much joy her mere presence gives me.

What material adds strength to anything or in this case person it touches? What healed my relationship scars and stopped the emotional bleeding; leaving me plenty of love to lavish on her? What material gives us the hardness to endure whatever life has in store? The answer my dear is your name, PORCELAIN. It may not be a name I'll ever call you, but it represents everything you mean to me. Everlasting beauty, uncompromising integrity, enduring strength, delicate femininity, and most importantly an intrinsic value that can only be measured by my ever increasing love for you.


Created by me for you, with all my heart,


Jim

# Chapter Forty-One

## Breakfast for Three

Marcel located one of the hidden keys in the yard of the Bainbridge mansion. The fluorescent light of the full moon made the simple task easier, as she had spent more than a few nights in the comfort of her friend's home.

Theirs' was an unusual relationship, a special bond. It began as friends, stopping just short of lovers, but continuing on to a higher level of intimacy. Her spirits lifted as she entered the gourmet kitchen. She remembered the wonderful meals he had prepared for her. The cozy nights cuddled in front of one of the many fireplaces, sipping wine or hot chocolate. The long walks on the park-like grounds, holding hands and discussing each other's future. Yes, this was a very special place and he a very special man.

She was exhausted having worked several days in a row. It was the downside of being a new flight attendant. The upside of all the travel was a boost to her freelance modeling career. Grabbing a quick snack, she climbed the back stairs and started down the hall toward his luxurious master suite. She was a quick, warm shower away from the loving arms of her friend.

She was stopped in her tracks by the unmistakable symphony of passion; the sound of lovemaking. She listened for a moment smiling, actually shedding a tear of joy for her lonely friend. It had been more than a year since he enjoyed the comfort of a woman. He did everything with so much love. He deserved some love in return. She turned on her heels and entered one of the bedrooms at the end of the hall. She smiled when she realized that she had chosen the room of his youngest son, her favorite. Selecting a T-shirt from a dresser drawer, she dove into bed and quickly drifted off to sleep.

I awoke to a sunlit room and the wonderful smell of my favorite meal. I assumed that since the other side of the bed was empty, that my new girlfriend was showing off her culinary skills. However, that bubble was quickly burst upon seeing the confused, suspicious and borderline angry face of my girlfriend returning from the bathroom. "I thought you said your kids weren't going to be home" the face said. "They aren't". I said, feeling a bit nervous, immediately sensing complexity of the situation. Grabbing the bull by the horns, I jumped up and found a robe to cover the beautifully long legs that glamorized one of my T-shirts. I threw on some sweats and taking her hand said "come with me, there is someone I want you to meet."

We entered the kitchen and found Marcel at the business end of the center island. She was the source of those seductive aromas of breakfast. I immediately announced our presence. "Good morning Marcel, this is my new girlfriend Simone." Marcel was a vision in the bright morning light. Her hair was loosely arranged in an up do. She was covered more by confidence than the football jersey of my son's that she wore. Just a hint of her cheeks were evident when she moved. The mounting tension threatened to replace the delicious aroma of breakfast. Just then Marcel announced cheerfully without turning "Sit down, breakfast is almost ready."

We sat. With the pressure only temporarily abated; Marcel turned and calmly placed a platter of hash browns and sausage on the counter. Suddenly the eyes of my exotic lover flashed, as she had reached the boiling point. She yelled. "Who is she?!" Marcel answered nonchalantly with her back turned, still focused on her task. "My name is Marcel." "Jim is my best friend." Finally, she turned holding a platter of scrambled eggs with cheese and Belgian waffles. Wearing a warm but, sly smile, she added "I'm not a threat to you, but if he were my man, he wouldn't be walking upright this early in the morning." We both sat stunned, basking in the aroma of breakfast. Marcel walked around the island put her arms around both of us. Kissing me on the cheek, she said "it's good to see you again". Marcel turned and kissed my new lover on the cheek and uttered the following "take good care of him, he deserves it." Marcel smiled and quickly turned and bounded across the floor, a bit of buttock revealed with each step. Then stopping at the base of the stairs, she chirped "I've got a plane to catch; enjoy your breakfast." Marcel showered and left without reappearing.

Back in the kitchen we ate quietly, actually ravenously. Finally my new lover, totally disarmed said "your friend is a really good cook." "I agree." I said with a full mouth.

We never directly discussed Marcel again. Although on occasion, I was asked if I had heard from any of my "old friends". It is true that Marcel wasn't a threat to our relationship, but women like Marcel linger in the minds of women. They can't help but feel the pressure. The relationship didn't last. I knew it wouldn't. There was nothing I could do to save it. On the plus side, I had finally moved on.

## Circle of Love

I give this gold chain to you,

'Cause it's gonna look hot.

Though it wraps around you,

Binding is the one thing it's not.

It has a dual purpose,

Like the lyrics of a good love song.

It has a serious message,

While spicing up your thongs.

It reminds me of you,

Strong and yet so soft.

It represents our love, so you must never take it off.

It may be made of metal,

But like our love it's precious and fragile.

And no matter how old it gets it'll never lose its value,

I give to you the most important thing I've got,

To keep you warm, maybe get you hot.

Designed to be worn in your secret place,

To keep me with you all the while, put a smile on your face.

It's not meant to define our love,

Just a reminder it's always there,

As it lies there, shimmering amongst your sexy underwear.

J.R. Russell

Sleepless

I went to bed, but no rest did I find.

Thoughts of you raced across my mind.

I longed for your softness,

I missed your sweet sounds.

Before you I was lost,

But since you I've found.

A sense of serenity,

Truth in your eyes,

The warmth in your heart,

I feel between your thighs.

When I'm inside you, I feel such peace,

And a revived feeling of confidence with every release.

I forget completely that my life has gone south,

When you sigh and give thanks, when I cum in your mouth.

I hope I give back what you want and need,

With all my heartfelt words, actions, and deeds.

My goal is to relax, energize, and brighten your eyes,

When I slurp juices from between your thighs.

I help you with problems that you have with school,

This time in love, I hope I'm not the fool.

There's a part of you that wants to be sexy and free,

That's why I caress and undress you, where others can see.

I knew it when our first conversation began,

That I was what you needed, in terms of a man.

You're certainly not the first,

But I pray you're the last.

'Cause when you're with me, my future is bright,

And I'm no longer haunted by my dark, dismal past.

These thoughts and others ran around in my head.

While I lay sleepless, without you in bed.


For my Lizzy; inspired by passion, written with love.


James Robert Russell

## Birthday Wishes for an Ex-Lover

Despite the fact that your heart once mine, has sadly moved on.

Bitter cold and darkness replacing a bright and sunny dawn.

The bond between us severed by a tightly shut door.

Leaving shared dreams like snowflakes, scattered on the floor.

I take the opportunity on this your special day.

To send my heartfelt hopes for happiness and prosperity your way.

For you I wish all the wonderful things, this year may have in store.

Happy 48<sup>th</sup> birthday and least that many more.

You are still loved, missed and thought of often.

Yours always,

Jim

# Venom

Venom: the debilitating, cancerous, poison courses through your veins.

The bitter condition of loneliness, its all too common name.

It torments and consumes you, so precious little remains.

Delivered by the concealed fangs of a dispassionate dame.

Your soul it does eat; the very essence of you.

It causes you to question everything you do.

Spirit draining, your mind struggling to keep pace

Again you find yourself in this desolate place.

How did you get there? That's what you'd like to know.

The last thing you remember is basking in love's glow.

That must be it! The binding common thread.

The emotions that can both exalt and make you wish you were dead.

Only under the guise of love do you let her get close.

Surrender yourself, let your guard down.

Before you realize what's happened, she's delivered her dose.

She leaves you to wander emotionally lost, never to be found.

Bruised, bewildered and terminally sad.

Feeling once again, that you've been had.

You're home alone, you address is pain.

Put there by the venom of the dispassionate dame.

James Robert Russell

# Chapter Forty-Six

## Eclipse

This story is a about an incident that happened to me during very tough times of illness and business reversals. It falls under the category of one time encounters. One of the rare, chance meetings that you hope you never forget. Now that I have written it down and shared it with you; I have insured that it will not be lost.

During those times, I was employed as a car salesman to help defray my medical expenses. It will suffice to say that I was not terribly successful at this position. Not necessarily because of my skills. Let's just say I was in moral conflict. It was important to me that the customer was happy. Not exactly the recipe for making a lot of money in the car business. There was however one magical October when all the stars and planets aligned, and I was having a great month. Lead salesman actually, I had sold six cars over the previous weekend to get to twenty-nine, but not one since. It was the following Saturday near closing time and I was scheduled off on Sunday and Monday, the last two days of the month. Time was running out.

Just then an elderly gentleman walked into the dealership. He was wearing dirty construction clothes. It was our practice to take walk-in leads in rotation. It wasn't close to being my turn, but for some reason everyone passed on helping him. It you knew the term that was used for late day walk-ins you'd understand why. I asked him if he needed help. He told me a story about his grand-niece. Everyone in the distance was laughing because the story looked like it was going to be a long one. He was living up to the vile nickname. He continued his story telling me how proud he was of his grand-niece that he never named. She worked so hard. She had straight A's in college, worked two part-time jobs, and helped take care of his ailing wife. The college was a forty-five mile drive each way. He wanted to get her a car that was good on gas and dependable.

He decided he wanted a new one because it would have a warranty. But it had to be the cheapest one we had. No frills, he said, he didn't want to "spoil her". I had two kids in college at the time, both athletes. I identified with her struggles.

By the time I had located and written up our "value leader"; which we technically weren't supposed to sell, it was seven-fifteen and everyone but the Sales and Finance managers were gone. She had requested a red car with a sunroof and a good sound system. This one was yellow, no A/C, manual shift, no floor mats, no radio. I told him that the car was scratched and we could get another one in by Monday, but I couldn't guarantee the color. It was fine with him, as long as the price was the same. I knew we could trade another dealership for a red one. At least she would get one thing that she wanted. The elderly gentleman paid cash and left saying that she would be back on Monday to pick up the car.

Upon leaving, the sales manager informed me that it was my thirtieth car of the month and it also virtually locked up the Salesman of the Month bonus. The bonus, plus the twenty percent override on all previous sales meant an extra $3000.00 this month. I had forgotten about the magnitude of the incentives, being so engrossed in the old man's story. The sales manager told me to take an extra day off. He would assign someone to deliver the car on Monday.

I received a phone call on Monday morning from the sales manager. He said that the car that the dealership traded for was $900.00 more expensive than the one we sold. The car contained the dealer installed sun and sound package. This package cost the dealership $500.00 and was comprised of a CD sound system, sunroof and color coordinated floor mats. I told him that I would pay for the difference out of my commission. Things go well for you when you do the right thing, I thought.

I returned to the dealership on Wednesday, expecting the veteran salesmen to tease me about being Salesman of the Month. Instead all the talk was about the woman that picked up the car and how grateful she was. The stories got better all day, even the women in the office said that she was "something". "Wait until you see her", they said. I took it all in stride figuring that this was their way of getting back at me. The joke was coming. They said that she was going to return later this week to thank me in person. For the uninitiated, guys will go through a lot of trouble to setup a joke like this. So when I returned to the dealership on Saturday after a day off and the buzz was that she had been in the dealership the previous day looking better than before, I knew the trap was being set.

The day passed quietly. I was at my desk waiting for the clock to release me. Then from across the showroom I heard the booming voice of one of the salesman saying, "He's here today." Then two other salesmen pointed in my direction, as if remotely controlled, saying, "He's over there." When I looked up to see what the commotion was, she was rounding the corner with a flourish that would make a super model jealous. Long, athletic limbs flowed fluidly, gracefully, but definitely purposefully. She walked with the confidence of a woman ten years her senior. She was clad in a high-collared, straight, grey wool dress that fell just below the knee. She wore the sheerest of hose that accentuated her long athletic legs; while her statuesque frame was supported by a pair of ankle strap stilettos that rendered only her feet naked in this stylishly mature ensemble.

Taking her direction from the now mannequin-like salesmen; she turned her focus in my direction. She looked downward as she walked, but I noticed perfection in her medium brown complexion. Her face was adorned only by giant silver hoop earrings and perfectly painted cranberry lips. I wanted to look away, but I couldn't. The soft wool shapeless dress that the designer intended to hide a woman's curves was failing miserably in its task. Her fingers and toes, wearing the same cranberry color were obvious warning signs of the approaching danger. When my glance returned to her face, I received the knockout punch. She had dark, thick wavy shoulder length hair that seemingly blew in her personal breeze, generated by an unseen machine. The locks framed her face perfectly and magnified the effect of her now visible pearl grey eyes. They seemed to be lit from within. That combined with the expression on her face was paralyzing. She was beautiful, dangerous and approaching me. You could summarize the scene by saying old enough to be legal, young enough to be lethal. I was in serious trouble.

I stood in front of my desk with my hand extended in friendship, attempting to look unaffected. I was hit with the gale force breeze of the incredible scent of essential oils, as she approached. Her purposeful gait never slowed, and with her last step she expertly stepped inside my stance. Her muscular but soft left thigh found its mark. Her arms reached inside my offer of a handshake with her hands palms up, sliding around my mid section and up my back, finally cupping her hands over my shoulders. I braced for impact.

Her body hit me with the force of a freight train made of marshmallow. Each part of her body landed individually, distinctively. First her right hip, then in rapid fire succession mid-section, the left then right breast. Her bottom lip fit between mine, which were locked in surprise, I imagine. Her top lip engaged mine with a slight sucking sensation, completing the docking maneuver. Her hair brushed across my shoulders and her earrings bounced off of my cheeks in whiplash reaction to the collision. It was the longest eight seconds of my life. Releasing me from her velvety vise-like embrace, she then cupped my face in her warm supple hands and I saw her cranberry accented lips and pearlescent teeth form the words; "Thank you for my car." I don't know if she actually voiced them or not. But I do know that if I had heard them, I probably would not be able to sleep to this day.

She smiled as she stepped back, seemingly pleased with her work, and placed ten of the most femininely formed fingers in my chest and played a single staccato piano note. The music was generated by the collection of silver bangles on her wrist that somehow I hadn't previously noticed. She turned and walked away, and I did the only thing a man in my condition could do. I fell back to a seated position on my desk.

She withdrew taking that intoxicating scent with her. Light slowly returned to the showroom and time started once again. As oxygen replaced her essence in my lungs; my brain gradually regained its composure.

From my seated position, I could see that the dress failed to hide her curves from this angle as well. I admired how her form made the soft wool dance in a manner that not even the donor lambs could accomplish. I realized at that moment that she was a rare phenomenon; a perfect storm of genes, age and execution. She may never be more stunning than she was that day. I hope not, for she was too much for mere mortal man. A young man couldn't handle her. An older man wouldn't survive her. You looked at her in amazement and awe. Knowing that this would be a once in a lifetime occurrence. You hold her in the reverence and fear that she deserves; knowing that too long of a look could mean blindness. A touch by the unworthy could turn them to stone. I never knew her name, but then again they don't name the rare Eclipse.

# Chapter Forty-Seven

## Questions

The game of love is simply a series of questions. A round of hide and seek. It is a quest for an answer to that ever burning question; a question that is actually several mysteries in one. We aim for the bulls-eye of a constantly moving target. We are armed with faulty equipment; a jaundiced eye, chemically altered thought processes (internally or externally or some combination of both), a time healed heart, and over active hormones. We depend on wounded egos, damaged self esteem and information that comes to us in the form of lies and innuendo to reach our ultimate and primal goal. The decision of a lifetime is ultimately based on hope, serendipity and happenstance. That question is love. Do I love him or her? Or more importantly; do they love me?

Our biggest enemy in this process is the mind. The mind seeks information, answers to the questions. We often rely upon these facts to make our decisions on what we think about a person and judge their opinions about us. Let's be frank, the brain sets us up to fail. Where is origin of the idea to have or buy that potential someone an alcoholic drink while talking "to get to know someone?" That single personality altering act forever taints the results of the question and answer session. Additionally, the meeting and resulting conversation is fueled and its course dictated by hormones introduced into our systems by you guessed it, the brain.

The brain also misleads us. Its primary goal is to gain facts, so questions are developed to access information in the other person's memory banks. The brain is satisfied with the conversation because it has attained "facts" for us to use to make a decision about the worthiness and interest level of this new discovery. The truth is that these "facts" are useless information because of the altered state of both the donor and the receiver. Moreover, the validity of "facts" is relative. Whether innocently or purposefully "facts" can be overstated, misinterpreted, left out, or simply lied about. Without an established baseline who's to know.

This is further evidenced by the recent trend toward electronic systems to help us find a mate. The mind is satisfied by this procedure because the format appeals to the mind's logic. We feel that if we analyze information and pictures that come from an electronic source, it must be true. The flaw in this methodology is that we spent time searching and analyzing information offered to us by people who have the same flaws that we ignore about ourselves. Do you think potential suitors take the time to analyze themselves, indentify their weaknesses and reveal them to the world in their profile? I think not.

The brain goes about its mission the only way it knows how, by thinking and evaluating the person's thought process. The reality is we don't really care. What we really want to know is what that person _feels_ about us. An example is, when a man asks a woman how old she is (other than legal reasons) he really wants to know how she _feels_ about a man his age. Why do you think that a perfectly rational person can repeatedly enter into relationships that are obviously inadequate, if not dangerous to them?

As humans we'd like to think that our relationships or attractions are based on something more substantial than "feelings", but in reality they're not. The fact that we put so little emphasis on the importance of our feelings is actually the main blockade to "true happiness". We unsuccessfully try to fill an emotional, physical void with intellect. We don't ride a rollercoaster because it makes sense to do so. We ride them because of the thrill that the ride produces. In many ways relationships are similar to the process of riding a roller coaster. You watch it from a distance to see how it operates and determine if it looks like fun. You study it, assess its design and build quality. The reaction of others to it is also quantified. Really, who wants something no one else wants? The anticipation and apprehension grows as you're strapped in for the ride of your life. Anxious moments are replaced by exhilaration, ups and downs, queasiness, excitement, sheer terror and hopefully satisfaction with minimal pain. If the excitement outweighs the pain and terror; you've got the makings of a relationship. You take that ride over and over again as the relationship grows. Hopefully some of the terror is removed, leaving sufficient excitement however to warrant continuing the bond. As the relationship matures, which varies in its timeframe, the brain comes back to life and re-assumes its role, but the problem is the brain wasn't involved in the relationship building process. It asks perfectly rational questions about the validity of the bond. These concrete bombshells usually have a devastating effect on the fragile chemical, emotional, physical chain you've developed. Its ill-timed actions have the power to sabotage a potentially beneficial relationship.

The final and most devastating blow to the emotional body is upon the break-up of the relationship. The mind's relentless pursuit of facts is in direct conflict with the body's need to heal. The mind's response to the break-up is to look at pictures for clues, analyze phone calls, and replay experiences to determine what it thinks is the cure for the pain. The answer to the question WHY?

The reality is that the emotional body doesn't want to know WHY? It doesn't help the healing process to know. In fact, the knowledge of why the relationship ended will inevitable cause more pain in the form of self-doubt, regret and the overwhelming need to explain or justify one's actions to someone who is no longer interested. No, the only thing that will help at this point is to hide away in some dark recess, either physically or emotionally depending on personality type. The brain's quest for knowledge hammers at the mid-section of the emotional body like a fighter with his opponent trapped in the corner. The brain levies a barrage of punches, all finding their mark, inflicting pain.

Questions such as: What did I do wrong? Do you think they'll come back? Soften you up for the knockout blows. Rhetorical questions like. Why did they leave me? Is there someone else? Did they ever really love me? The potential answers to these and other questions asked by the mind are far more painful than the actual break-up. The pain inflicted by these and other mysteries is what cause even the most of rational people to cry out to God or anyone that will listen to their plight. The combination of fond memories, unanswered questions, crushed dreams and the feeling of betrayal are what lengthen the required "mourning period" before you can safely and productively move on to a new relationship.

The real tragedy is that some people never really move on. The fact is everyone is affected by the quality and the nature of the relationships they've had in their lives. There is a theory that we are born with great personality traits and qualities which are nurtured and grow within us. However, bad experiences cause us to grow protective layers like an onion. The good in us remains and grows within, but is covered by more and more layers as time goes on. Outsiders can see the good, but can only benefit from what is allowed to seep through the protective layers of fear of commitment and resistance to vulnerability. Time can slowly peel away these layers, but it is delicate process. It can be said that we don't really interact with a person; rather we deal with the layer of defense that they are currently displaying.

Deception

Being a victim of deception is the cruelest pain of all

Heartstrings strained like an archer's bow

You're setup to take the fall

Held securely, bound by your deepest fear

They hide the things you need to know

Say what you long to hear

Creating images of love, illusions in your mind

They illuminate shadows of doubt

Steadily reassuring, pretending to be kind

The burning fever consumes you

Brought on by the disease

Sadly you accept your fate, see their point of view

Lying there motionless, guts swollen in pain

Hurt much more by their indifference

You realize your love's been given in vain

If you dare to ask, they're certain to confess

For them it is not about love

It's simply the need to possess

James Robert Russell

## No Pain, No Pleasure

My story would not be complete if it did not include some of the more unpleasant moments as well. A few of the incidents have been included in earlier stories, these are all new. Some of the characters may have been introduced earlier, others not. See if you can determine who's who. They will be described as accurately as possible without negativity, judgment or venom, all while maintaining their anonymity. In some cases, the memories are still very painful.

### Tickets! Tickets! Who has tickets!

My freshman year of college; a time for discovery; a time to adjust. I wasn't able to go away to college like most of my friends, so enrolling in a predominately white college after attending all-black schools, was an adjustment that I would have to make on my own. Admittedly, it was lonely. Additionally, I worked full time, so there was no real college life to speak of. I ate lunch in different places around campus hoping to meet new friends. Two months went by without measurable results, until that memorable day. After finishing my lunch, I sat on a bench near the tennis courts. It was a rare warm November day. I must have dozed off because I was awakened by the sound of tennis balls being struck with violent intensity. I was surprised to see the alarmingly beautiful creature responsible for all the commotion. She was tall, about six feet. She was wearing a tennis skirt that made her muscular legs seem even longer, if that was possible. She was a ballerina with a tennis racket. Picture the Williams sisters with the visage of Vanessa Williams. I sat in amazement as she struck ball after ball with power and accuracy. When she gathered her belongings and walked in my direction I said without planning, "When will you be here again, I enjoyed watching you." Smiling she said, "I'll be here tomorrow at two if the weather holds." She never broke stride. I called after her saying, "I'll bring you a hot dog." I didn't know if she heard me, but I regretted saying it.

The following day was warm. I ate on the same bench by the tennis courts and waited anxiously. At exactly 2 pm, she walked down the winding path toward the courts. When she was about 10 feet away I said, "Hi!" She replied with a look of confidence, "Did you bring my hot dog?" Without thinking whether she was making fun of me, I answered. "I brought you two." She stopped in her tracks and turned to look at me in amazement. Then smiling she said, "It's going to be a short workout today." I waited.

Our conversation after her workout was spirited, competitive, and I am pretty sure I impressed her. I was actually amazed that I could speak. She told me she had graduated in June and was soon going on the Pro Tour. She was more woman than I had ever encountered to date. I don't know who was more shocked when I asked her out, as she stood to leave. There was a sold-out concert on Friday; the hottest ticket in town. She contemplated the offer for about fifteen seconds and accepted. I asked her to pick-up the tickets in will call for me; I had to work the day shift on Friday. She agreed and gave me her address and instructions to pick her up at seven.

Emotionally, Friday came quickly. I was ready, at least in spirit. I wore a black three piece suit with a wide collar, ivory crepe shirt. The outfit was completed by black suede stack heeled shoes with ivory piping. Hey! It was the seventies!! I arrived at her door on time, and after a second knock a girl about my age came to the door, opened it and just stared at me. Finally, without changing her expression she said, "Wait here, I'll get my sister" and closed the door. I was suddenly very nervous, and questioning the wisdom of the whole idea. My date appeared at the door finally, sporting a colorful silken kimono. She was wearing makeup, but her hair was still in rollers, covered by a scarf. I stepped toward the door, but her eyes stopped me cold. They weren't angry, but they weren't inviting either. She leaned forward and planted one of the sweetest kisses on my lips that I had ever felt. As she retreated, she shook her head sideways and slowly closed the door. She never broke eye contact and they delivered the remainder of the message that the kiss started. She would be going to the concert with my tickets, but not with me. I quickly did the math. I was a very young eighteen and she was a mature twenty-one. I had been had, but I didn't feel so bad. Those eyes, that kiss, it was a mercy killing. Lesson learned.

Holidays have always been a sore spot for me in relationships. They are where the rubber meets the road, so to speak. This one was no exception.

## Valentine's Day Massacre

Being on the fast track and making your mark in corporate America requires certain sacrifices and tough decisions. I was ordered by the company president to make a trip to Grand Rapids for a very important sales meeting on Friday. It was scheduled to be an all day affair ending at about 9pm. The instructions, get the contract or else. This sudden directive changed our plans for Friday, Valentine's Day. I tried to explain it to her, but she wasn't being at all cooperative. I was separated and waiting for my divorce to go through and she was losing her patience, I guess. I offered to change our plans to Saturday. No response. I really felt bad about it, but it couldn't be helped.

The meeting ended successfully at about eight-thirty. Instead of celebrating with my colleagues, I decided to drive back home and surprise her. I was able to locate the requisite roses, I even purchased champagne and chocolate covered strawberries to go with the gift I already had purchased for her. I made the typically six-hour drive in good time considering the rain and fog.

It was just about 4am, as I fumbled with the lock to her apartment. Upon entering, I put the champagne and strawberries in the refrigerator and headed to her room with the flowers and her gift. Maybe I was too exhausted to notice or maybe I just don't think that way. Something should have registered; something should have stopped me from seeing what I was about to see. But it didn't. I felt a sense of doom, but I had no idea why. I was removing my coat as I entered her bedroom, so I didn't see them right away. Yes, them! She and her ex-boyfriend were sleeping comfortably. I was in shock; so much so that I just sat down in a chair across the room. I must have sat there fifteen minutes just watching them sleep. Finally, having exhausted every brain cell and regained my ability to breathe, I switched on a lamp and waited. She began to stir after a minute or so, then waking she sat up abruptly, arousing her ex-boyfriend. The terror in their eyes was obvious and justified, but I sat calmly contemplating my next move. Just then she spoke, saying the worst possible thing she could out of a thousand inadequate responses. "What are you doing here?" She shrilled.

Now I was angry. Caught in the act of the ultimate betrayal, she asks me why I'm there. Her boyfriend, sensing my mood change starts to squirm. A man is never more defenseless than he is without his pants on. I motion for him to leave, as I stand and walk towards the living room. In less than two minutes, he is scurrying thru the living room, apologizing as he went. "My quarrel is not with you" I said, as he went through the door.

My emotions had caught up with me by the time she sheepishly appeared in the living room. I was hurt, no devastated, but still fuming about the betrayal. The lack of respect. The lack of decency, she could have at least gone somewhere else. I had a key for goodness sake! No one should have to see what I had just seen. Those who have had the misfortune of being in my position know exactly what I mean. Those of you who haven't; count your blessings. Your retinas and memory banks are permanently scarred by the sight. Unfortunately, this would not be the last person that would cause me to have to endure this type of pain. At one time, I thought it was a reflection on me. But later after many hours of wrestling with the issue, I determined someone's infidelity had nothing to do with me. I was just who they were. However, that realization did nothing to ease the pain.

She stood across the room from me, silently glaring at me attempting to assess my mood. I gave her no response other than to rise and walk past her to leave the apartment. I didn't even say goodbye. I knew that I couldn't stand to look at her another moment. Her apparent lack of emotion angered me as much as the betrayal.

I sat in my car waiting for the windows to defog and my head to clear. I was no longer angry. I have always maintained that anger is not an emotion. Rather it is a reaction to a "true emotion." In this case, the truth was that I was hurt and disappointed. Just then there was banging at the passenger side window, as I was putting the car in reverse. I lowered the window only far enough to see the drenched face of my ex-lover standing in the cold pouring rain. She had run out in an attempt to "explain" what had happened. My heart hardened with each failed attempt at rationalizing her actions. She couldn't even finish ridiculous statements like. "It wasn't my fault." "He just came over." "You weren't here." "It won't happen again." "I love you." The meaningless words fell from her lips like the torrents of rain drops from the early morning sky. I continued to back out of the parking space without uttering a sound. As I pulled away, she banged on the trunk in frustration and ran bare-foot in her now totally saturated bathrobe after my car, begging for another chance. My heart softened for a second, and I stopped the car allowing her to catch-up. I exited and she hugged me, look-ing up with huge tear filled brown eyes. "Please give me another chance?" She weakly, but sincerely asked. I broke free from her grip without speaking and got back into my car and drove away. In retrospect, the scene was poignant, but I was wise not to be moved by its drama.

The worst part of betrayal to me is the lie. The discovery of a lie is insidious; it eats away at the very foundation of a relationship. Everything hereto for accepted as truth is put into question by the utterance of one lie. It not only breaks the bond of trust; it makes me feel that you think I'm stupid as well, and will believe any-thing. The truth is that I would, but only because with love comes an unshakeable belief. Everyone has different tolerance levels, but relationships rarely survive multiple lies.


I Saw What You Did Last Night


It was my turn to suffer. I was caught in the very sticky web of agony and apprehension. The glue was love and the fear of loss. The problem: waiting for her divorce to finalize. It had been almost a year of negotiations and delays. I knew the drill. I had endured three different separations and many acrimonious settlement attempts, before I finally was divorced. That knowledge generated compassion for a situation that was totally unacceptable to me. She, to her credit did everything she could to justify my wait.

It had been a long work week, and because it was Friday she wasn't available. I sat in the car mulling over my problems in the parking lot of a local cocktail lounge frequented by young professionals. It was a rare feeling, but I needed a drink. I was walking through the dark parking lot toward the lighted doorway of the club, when I was literally sucker punched in the stomach by the sight of her tall silhouette, accompanied by her husband exiting the club. The sight actually forced me to lean on the trunk of a parked car or I'm sure I would have hit the ground. It is amazing how much you can put out of your mind, if you are never confronted with the truth. The truth in this case had sent my heart plummeting to a depth that I didn't know my torso contained. It didn't help that she was wearing the same black dress that she wore to dinner with me last week. I had watched her put it on and helped her take it off afterwards. That wonderful memory now haunted me. The only saving grace was that she didn't look happy.

After several minutes, I regained my composure and realized how ridiculous the entire situation had become. I was jealous and hurt because I saw my girlfriend out on a date with her husband!!! I wanted to slap myself. I knew what I had to do.

I went directly to the phone when I got home, some three hours later. The red light on my answering machine was flashing furiously. An urgent message was waiting for me. While flipping through the phone book for the number of the County Records Department, I heard this message. "I'm so sorry I couldn't meet you this evening." "My husband insisted on meeting to talk about "our future" she said with disgust. "I'll meet you tomorrow at three to make it up to you." "I love you." I smiled, but those three little words weren't going to stop me from doing what I should have done long ago.

Admittedly, the county she lived in made it very tough to get a divorce. The guidelines were particularly brutal to successful men. I myself struggled in this system, and didn't get divorced until my ex-wife and I moved to another county that favored a father's rights to his children. My heart began to pound as I dialed the number to the Automated Record Service. Its pace increased, as I scrolled through the menu to find divorce fillings. I sat to enter their information after each prompt, which was difficult to hear over the ever increasing din of my heartbeat. I took a breath before I hit the nine key, the search prompt. I didn't breathe again. The mechanical sounding woman's voice had delivered the final blow. No existing record; the voice said over and over. I slowly hung up the phone.

She arrived the next day at precisely 3 pm wearing heels, thigh high hose, a trench coat and a smile. She intended to make good on her promise. She kissed me as she removed the coat. She thought the smile I gave her was in appreciation of her outfit, admittedly she did look incredible, but the words I uttered sent her reeling and made her feel suddenly, uncomfortably naked. Calmly I said, "I saw you last night." She tearfully explained both her dilemma and her commitment to me. She had to negotiate with him, he wouldn't let go. I delivered the crushing blow. "Negotiate what? You haven't even filed for divorce!" She told me how much she loved me, saying that "She didn't want to lose me." She wanted desperately to show me and I let her. She even left the clothes she had in the car with me and went home naked in an attempt prove her allegiance to me.

In the beginning, by accepting the unacceptable, I had set myself up for destruction. During the next year whether intentional or not; she dished out more pain to both her husband and myself than anyone should have to bear. It has been said that a boy once asked a wise elder "How does a man learn to carry a burden that is too heavy for him to bear". The answer; "One pound at a time."

Work to Do

Our relationship had just begun to settle down, from the unsustainable pace that we had maintained in the beginning. After five months of unbridled passion, a bit of normalcy had taken hold and exposed the kind of relationship that we could hope to sustain. It

149

was a good relationship with promise; she was the kind of woman that could make you want to marry her quickly. Fortunately, I am patient and most importantly cautious.

She called me to tell me that there was a medical emergency in her family. She needed to go away for the weekend. On Sunday, I decided that I would surprise her by completing one of the items on a "to do" list we had recently created for her home. It was a one day landscaping upgrade of her front yard. I had completed about thirty minutes of digging, enough to work up a pretty good sweat. I was standing back from the house mentally picturing the new arrangement when I heard from my right the unmistakable sound of the bark of her two hundred pound dog. He was normally in the garage, but this bark was definitely outside. Terrified, I looked in the direction of the sound to view something that was equally wounding. He saw me before she did. He was walking her dog, providing me with sufficient evidence of their attachment. Additionally, as if I needed more evidence, she gasped upon seeing me with her hands in front her face, revealing a rather large engagement ring; the smoking gun.

She conveniently walked away with the dog, while he introduced himself. I did the same, explaining that I was a handy man she had contracted to do some repairs. He was not the home repair type I surmised, but he wanted to review the list. I went to my truck and quickly scratched number four "fuck Lisa" from the list we had finalized just a few days earlier.

After reviewing the list and observing my work, he went into the house and returned with Lisa and a generous check to cover the work. He shook my hand saying, "I'm sure this should cover everything. Lisa has convinced me that you are trustworthy, and will finish the job." I assured him that I would. He shook my hand again and asked if I could come back tomorrow, as he would soon be leaving for the airport to catch a flight back to Europe on a long term assignment. I glanced toward Lisa and noticed that her unusually large brown eyes that once possessed the power to change the course of rivers now looked drained and terrified. She took my hand in both of hers and weakly said, "Thank you, Thank you for everything." I retorted. "You can thank me when the work is done." I left hurt, but smiling. Lisa called out after me "I will."

You may wonder why I took the high road. Why didn't I expose her and make a scene? Well, the answer is simple; it wouldn't make me feel any better. Additionally, I didn't do anything wrong. Why should I bear the added burden of ruining his day? It wasn't my job. Besides, I was sure he would find out about her soon enough anyway. One final answer to your obvious question. Of course I cashed the check and did the work on the list. Did that include number four? I'll never tell.

### Shhhh!

Several years after my divorce, I returned to the church that I attended while I was married. I had taken time away from the congregation because your friends, as well meaning as they try to be, always choose sides. I had returned to the church after giving the dust time to settle after the marital explosion. Things were of course different, for example I no longer had an assigned pew. The congregation was large and I had somehow managed not to run into anyone that I knew, a mixed blessing. As I non-chalantly stood in the vestibule waiting to be let into the sanctuary; I felt eyes upon me. Hoping that the eyes weren't accompanied by a disapproving leer, I looked around to try and find the source of the optical probing in my back. I was pleasantly surprised when I found a warm pair of medium brown eyes boldly staring at me over cheeks spattered with freckles. I quickly surmised that those brown eyes had taste to match their boldness, not because they had selected me out of the crowd. Rather, it was because of the stunning ensemble they had chosen to grace her slight, but feminine frame. The loose-fitting, ecru cashmere dress had a medium brown suede belt tossed haphazardly about her hips. The high, delicately rolled collar was a perfect base for her angular face, that was made up to blend beautifully with the ensemble; while simultaneously providing stark contrast to her stunning red hair; that was done in a simply elegant style that partly concealed the right side of her face. I nodded, she smiled. I returned my glance forward, as I walked into the sanctuary.

I could tell you that I didn't think about her during the service, but that would be a lie. I was mainly trying to remember who she was. Finally, near the end of the service, I remembered that she had been attending the church quietly for years, always alone. She belonged to the Usher Board, but other than that I really hadn't paid attention to her, until today. After all, I was married all of those years.

After the service, I was exiting the building after having had a pleasant conversation with a couple that my ex-wife and I had been friends with. I was leaving with a good feeling about the return visit, having been well received. I was just beginning to descend the tall flight of stairs leading to the sidewalk, holding the handrail, as it must have rained just a few minutes before.

As I stepped toward the second stair, a lilting, but confident contralto voice from behind me said. "Escort a lady to her car?" I turned and looked over my shoulder in time to glimpse a gloved right hand snap a brown umbrella to attention, as a bare and unadorned left hand slid neatly under my right arm. I noticed that she had added a subtly shimmering, full length, brown, lightweight silk topcoat to the ensemble that floated gracefully over the chocolate brown, suede pumps that completed the outfit.

She asked, as we reached the bottom of the stairs. "Did you enjoy the service?" Without waiting for an answer, she continued. "I'm glad to see that you've returned. Are you going to work with the Recreation Ministry again?" I replied, "I haven't decided just yet." "I am certain that they would love to have you back" she said. I had begun to comment when she interrupted me saying, "This is my car." She deftly unlocked the door and slid behind the wheel of a Mercedes convertible. "Great! It's stopped raining," she said excitedly. With that, she pushed a button activating the power top, reached for the dashboard; retrieved her sunglasses, which she put on with a flourish and handed me her business card while saying. "If you're ever in the downtown area call me, and we'll have lunch." I read the card aloud "Vice-President of Information Services" I smiled while nodding my approval, saying "I'm impressed." As she backed out of her parking space, she countered "So am I." She didn't bother to look back at me, because we both knew that I was going to call her.

On Tuesday morning, I called to see if she was available on Thursday for lunch. Her assistant answered the phone. "Good Morning, Ms Garrett's office" was the professional response. "Hello, Mr. Russell for Ms Garrett," I replied. "Oh! Mr. Russell," the voice traded its professionalism for congeniality instantaneously. "Ms Garrett is expecting your call." Expecting? I thought to myself. "Hello!" The excited voice said. She continued with a baby talk overtone. "I'm mad at you; well disappointed anyway." "You'll have to make it up to me" she continued. I sensed the playful mood and asked "What is it that I have done wrong?" "Wrong? I expected you to call yesterday! I would have if I had your number!" She exclaimed, with a bit of feigned indignation. "Sometimes a guy has to play it a little coy," I responded calmly. "Well coy doesn't work with me, I'm a what you see is what you get kind of girl", she exclaimed proudly.

"I'll try to remember that! Are you available on Thursday for lunch?" I inquired. She put the phone down; her voice was muffled, but I heard her say "Millie would you clear my Thursday afternoon schedule? That's right, everything after Walker. Also could you make reservations at "M" for one o'clock? Thank you." "M", I thought to myself, kind of... She interrupted my thought process, as she came back to the phone. "I'm free now!" She said cheerfully; meet me at "M" at one." Sensing and interpreting my silence, she said "the first date's on me." I wasn't insulted, I thought to myself. "I'm looking forward to it," I said. She ended the conversation with a sultry; "Bye, bye darling." I'm in trouble, I thought to myself, as I put my phone back in my pocket.

Thursday arrived quickly. I completed my appointment and arrived at "Metropolitan" at 12: 50. I had been there once before; the food was excellent, the service impeccable, the price outrageous. The reason she chose it I surmised was the décor, curved high backed booths arranged in random semi-circles affording maximum privacy. I was seated at a booth in the left rear of the room. This spot gave me a clear view of her as she entered. It was a crisp day in November, but she blew in like a windy day in May; the type of day when the wind seems to blow in all directions at the same time. The anatomical symphony that was her gait was accentuated by her classically beautiful outfit. Her movements were so wonderfully choreographed, each body part playing its singular role creating a dazzling, though subtle, visual extravaganza. I noticed that her frame wasn't as slight as I thought. She had more than her share of curves. Some poor woman had gone wanting. I thought to myself. She should have to carry a sign warning of "Dangerous Curves Ahead." She arrived at the table with both hands extended, saying "Sit, please sit!" "I'm sorry I'm late. I thought Walker would never shut up." After we sat, she reached out and took my hand in both of hers and said "You look great!" Her eyes lit up as much as her smile. Just then the waiter arrived, giving me time to notice her silver and white turquoise ringed right hand. The white stand-up collared blouse with barrel cuffs she wore was covered by a grey wool vest that simultaneously accented her bust and waist line. She ordered a martini and I, a Grey Goose and tonic. As the waiter left to fill our drink orders she crossed her legs, revealing the facts that the wide pleated, grey wool skirt had a concealed split and she was wearing black lace-topped thigh high stockings. Later during the meal, I would discover that she was also wearing sheer black net panties. The sign should have flashing lights! I thought to myself.

Our lunch was spirited; the conversation was lively, intense and intimate. The food was incredible, probably enhanced by the way she threw her legs across my lap, so she could sit closer while she cut and fed me asparagus. That's how I saw the panties, she pretended not to notice. She had Marilyn Monroe inspired mannerisms. Big eyes, gestures and expressions; she was brilliant, funny, overtly sexual and coy, all at the same time. On most women her actions might be considered over the top, but on her they seemed perfectly appropriate. Suddenly she gasped, after looking at my watch. "It's three-thirty, we have to go. I've ordered dessert and I have to get back to the office by four o'clock." This seemingly hair brained randomness was a trait that would endear me to her. She downed the last of her martini as we were walking to the door. I draped her cape about her shoulders, as she waved to the waiter, "The usual gratuity Michel," she called over her shoulder. Now it was my turn to be confused. The waiter answered back, "Merci Madame." I wasn't listening. She must have seen the questions written all over my face as we went through the door, because she helped me with my coat and then handed me the rose that she had taken from the table.

Still confused, I watched as she raised her hand, as if she were hailing a cab; an odd thing to do in Cleveland, as it is not considered to be a cab town. She turned to me and quickly explained that "the restaurant had her Corporate Card on file." "You're holding my souvenir of a wonderful first date," as she clutched my coat lapels and stood on her toes to kiss me gently. "What about dessert?" I asked. "It has just arrived," she explained. Just then a black Lincoln Town car pulled up, then while giving me a look I'll never forget, she said "I ordered my car so that we could make out on the way back." The driver opened the rear door and we entered, she, and the pleated skirt leaving nothing to the imagination. As soon as the driver closed the door; she was all over me, until we stopped in the basement parking garage of her office building. She exited the car, thanked the driver and acted as though she had returned from an important meeting until the elevator doors closed, when it started all over again. She stopped suddenly wagging her finger at me. She quickly reapplied lipstick, using the shiny stainless steel doors as a mirror; adjusted the "girls" in her vest and turned to look at me; still panting. "I want you to meet someone."

She walked quickly across the wide open office occupied by approximately thirty people. Stopping at a desk where a pleasant looking 40ish woman was seated. "Millie" she said, "This is Mr. Russell." We exchanged pleasantries. She continued, "Millie is my confident, you can tell her anything. If she gives you a message from me, treat it as if you heard me say it." "Millie, please give him one of your cards, and always put his calls through unless, I'm in a meeting with Walker, then forward it to my cell." She continued, "Millie could you please let the staff know that the meeting will start in ten minutes."

"Millie is indispensible," she said, softening her stance for the first time since she entered the building. As Millie walked away, she motioned to me "I want you to see my office, so that you may imagine me while I'm talking to you." Closing the door, she said "I have complete privacy here, a private restroom, dressing area, large comfortable furniture, soundproof walls and one-way glass." She pointed out each item, ending at the full wall of glass behind her desk which prompted me to quip "nice view". She glided around the room gracefully, but I knew this tour was important information. "I really hate to rush off" she said, "but they're waiting on me." "I had a wonderful time today" she said as she stood in front of the glass walls framed between the skyline and the lake.

As she spoke, I thought, she has a classic forties movie star look. I could only guess at her age, but she was probably slightly older than I, around fifty. However, she had the skin and a body that a thirty five year old would be proud to own. As I turned to leave, I said coyly. "I had a great time too, but I guess I'll be going. I don't want to hold you up." "Just like that!" She said in amazement, as she stepped toward me. I stopped and turned, looking her directly in the eyes as I approached. Upon reaching her, I quickly parted her grey wool skirt like the curtain at Carnegie Hall on opening night and tugged at her now damp black net panties. They offered no resistance, nor did she. As she stepped out of them, I said "I'll be taking these with me." "I like your style big fella;" she called after me, as I stuffed her panties in my coat pocket, and left her office.

I was able to reflect on my first encounter as walked to my car. No matter how much logic I tried to apply to the situation; the result was the same. I was totally out of control. So be it.

I received a call at home late that evening from a subdued version of the woman I had dined with earlier in the day. She sleepily cooed, purred, and baby talked through a ten minute call, a process we would later dub "lullabying." Just before ending the call, she asked if I could meet her for drinks tomorrow at six at Sarava. I agreed that I would.

Sarava was an upscale Brazilian themed restaurant bar that was frequented by the up and coming professional crowd. I was aware of it because my daughter was a chef there; the food was exotic and spicy, the Mojitos potent, the atmosphere electric. She looked ravishing; she smiled as I greeted the staff that I knew. My daughter immediately appeared with four tapas, featuring Sarava's specialties. The end of the week crowd was raucous; it was impossible to hear. We "communicated" via looks and touch. After just over an hour of "communicating" we decided to leave. On the way back to our cars, she apologized for having to leave, explaining that she had to change before a dinner function. She also apologized for wearing a pantsuit, saying that "it was so cold this morning". I replied, "No problem, you're lovely." She smiled and said "you're sweet, but I really wanted to show you my new panties" trying to maintain the upper hand in the relationship. It was a nice jab, but I quickly countered by giving her a little kiss and an abrupt spin. She looked back at me with a surprised look on her face. I continued, reaching around her waist, quickly unbuckling her belt, then unhooking and unzipping her pants. I then slid both hands down the back of her pants caressing her bare buttocks. Spinning her around again, I snapped the delicate waistband and said, silver lace thongs; very pretty. I left her standing in the parking lot next to her car, trying to hold her pants up. The excitement that my aggression caused was apparent on her face. She managed to utter desperately, "Call me?!"

The next six weeks passed quickly, seamlessly through Christmas. Our "encounters" had increased in frequency, intensity and variety. They included a polar expedition on a frozen beach, investigative reporting in the deserted stacks at the library, and a comparative study of nudes at the art museum. We experimented with camera angles at daytime matinees. Speaking of camera angles, she asked me to preview her upcoming webinar one Saturday; that was going to be broadcast from her office. She knew that I wouldn't understand the material, but she needed to practice in front of a camera. The webinar began innocently enough, but then just when my eyes were about to glaze over from the content; she wrote something on the white board and went off camera. She returned wearing fewer garments. This happened subsequently every five minutes or so until she was wearing only pumps and jewelry. The educational value of the broadcast never suffered. She ended by turning to face the camera and while winking she said, "I hope you enjoyed the show". "Thank you for "coming", as she winked slowly again." I had always wondered how my female teachers would have looked naked, while writing at the board. I now knew.

I received a call from Millie on Tuesday morning; we had become fast friends. I had even sent her flowers once, because she truly was indispensible. "Good Morning, Mr. Russell" she began professionally. "Ms Garrett would like you call her on her cell at eleven o'clock, and continue to call every five minutes until you reach her." "Is that the entire message Millie?" I asked. "That's it!" she replied. I thought I heard her giggle, as she hung up the phone. I did as I was instructed. At 12:30 having been unsuccessful in getting through to her; I called Millie. I explained to Millie that I called as she requested, but had been unsuccessful in reaching her. Millie answered cryptically, "I am quite certain that you did." Millie continued, "I routed her cell calls to her pager, she has been in a meeting since eleven." "She is wearing both devices in her panties. I'll put you through now; she just went into her office." The phone was answered hastily, unprofessionally. The panting voice said, "The meeting lasted much longer than I had planned." Before I could comment she continued, "I am sitting in my desk chair with my feet on the windows." First I heard the phone drop, and then I heard her loudly finish manually, what I had started electronically.

Admittedly, ours was an unusual relationship, but it was a good one. Without additional information you might think that the attraction was chemical, purely physical. The facts were that we had several things in common. We had both been divorced; twice in her case. We were intellectually and educationally balanced, we shared many similar interests and goals. We loved to travel and both of us enjoyed cooking, gardening and sports. I liked to say that were chemically bonded.

But most importantly, we respected each other's boundaries. Only twice did she come to my home unannounced; both times were in the same week. The first time was later that same Tuesday; well actually it was at three in the morning. She was frantically knocking on my door saying that she had had a terrible nightmare in which I had been critically injured. I opened the door to find her wearing only boots and a sheet draped around her. She rushed inside crying and shivering saying that "she desperately needed a hug." The other time was on Thursday, she arrived at my home at about six-thirty, after work. I prepared a quick dinner for us; it was a nice surprise actually, because I hate eating dinner alone. We were discussing our plans for Saturday night when suddenly her mood collapsed. She began to tear up, as she told me for the first time about her son that had "special needs". I listened intently while holding her hands, as she described how difficult it had been for so many years. He was currently institutionalized, but may be coming home soon for a short visit before switching to a new facility. She would of course be busy and need outside help during that time.

Then as quickly as it started, she stopped talking and insisted on clearing the dishes and such. I protested, but she wouldn't hear of it. Finally, I said, "at least let me get you an apron." "I don't need one" she called after me, as I ignored her and headed for the laundry room. After a minute or few of digging, I returned to the kitchen with an apron that would sufficiently protect her black knit dress to find her standing at the sink in nothing but her fire engine red silk bra and panties, black thigh high stockings and patent leather pumps. She looked ravishing, but her mood was still subdued, at least for her. Ladies, if you happen to see a seminar or article on how to keep a relationship fresh and exciting, hosted or written by A. Garrett, trust me, it is time or money well spent. I asked her with my hand on her shoulder, "Is there anything else I can do for you?" "Just keep me company," she said, attempting sexy, but only achieving tired. After finishing she kissed me on the cheek and reminded me again about Saturday night. She then slipped on her coat and picked up her dress, explaining that it was due to go to the cleaners, and left.

I didn't hear from her on Friday or Saturday, and I was glad because it gave me time to think. I was certain that there was something special about Saturday; she had mentioned marriage more than a few times in the last couple of weeks. She talked at length about being tired of this and that. She pointed out various aspects of being single, that really took their toll on you. We were scheduled to go the symphony and have a late dinner with some of the other executives of the company. This was a turning point in the relationship, I was certain. I wasn't ready to "pop the question myself," but I was prepared with an answer if she did.

I arrived at her home in formal attire on Saturday, and was greeted by her driver, this time with a limousine. The driver let me in the car, where she was waiting. The evening went just about as planned, with her playing the expected executive role. I had acquitted myself well with her colleagues; everything went as well as it possibly could. The ride home however was completely different. Not bad, mind you. She was just more like she usually was. We hadn't really "been together" in a week; the longest stretch we had endured. We had been limited to holding hands and sly remarks all evening. Now as she downed almost an entire bottle of champagne, the other side of her had returned. There was a lot of pent-up emotion that needed to be released. She was more out of her gown than in; by the time we arrived at her home. It was impossible for her to disguise her condition, as I walked her to the door. She was actually cute when she was drunk, her gestures and demeanor were grander; almost comical, while certainly less refined.

Upon entering the foyer, she knocked over a brass umbrella stand, which made quite a commotion. I chuckled as she turned, wagging her finger to scold me. "Shhhh, you're going to have to be quiet. She escorted me to the family room and said. "Have a seat, and a help a girl out." "Get out of some of those clothes, while I check on things upstairs." I smiled again, while watching her slowly make her way to the stairs. This is it, I thought to myself as I waited. Fifteen minutes later she returned much more composed, wearing a pearl gray satin gown with ivory lace trim, that covered everything, yet magnified every wonderful detail. She was carrying a small box, which she sat on the table in front of me and turned toward the kitchen. She returned with a bottle of champagne and two glasses. I asked "for me?" as I pointed to the box. She reached for the table and picked up the remote for the fireplace. Her sultry voice had returned and she said, "That depends on what you have for Mama," as she began to struggle with my pants. "I thought you were going to help me out?" she said, with more than a little frustration in her voice. "You take care of the champagne and I'll take care of this," she said as she looked hungrily at my crotch. After a toast and a couple of quick glasses; we ended up on the floor, again making a clattering noise, as the glasses were knocked to the floor. At first she laughed, followed by frustration in her face. "Shhhh! Now I have to go and check on him again."

"Get out of those pants!" she cooed excitedly. I did as I was commanded.

Passion was written all over her face when she returned, she quickly mounted me and began to work her magic. Just when she thought she was finished and had won; I flipped her over to "drive my point home" so to speak. Her cheeks were rosy as much from ecstasy as from the heat of the fireplace, and with each hammering stroke her theatrics grew louder and louder. I asked her "are you sure this is alright with your son home" as I felt her legs tighten around me in a vice like grip. "Keep fucking me!!" She shrilled. "My son isn't home silly. My husband is a light sleeper." I silently mouthed the word husband, as I frantically tried to free myself from her fleshy iron restraints. I could only imagine being shot in the back of the head as she pleaded, "Shhhh!! Please stay! Finish fucking me!!" It was my turn to run for the door, grabbing clothes as I went. As I closed the door I heard her tearfully cry out. "Call me?!"

I didn't hear from her on Sunday or Monday, nor did I go back to the church. She didn't call to offer an apology or excuse. However, I did wonder about myself. I didn't have much of a reaction to the situation. It was accepted as a foregone conclusion, like January snow in Cleveland. It was going to happen, and there was nothing you could do about it. So why complain? Had I become that calloused, that I didn't even expect long-term happiness anymore? Could anybody be trusted? Did anybody really care about **my feelings**?

On Tuesday morning I received a call at my office. The pleasant voice said "Mr. Russell, Ms Garrett would like you to call her cell at eleven o'clock and continue calling until you reach her." "Is that the entire message Millie," I said without emotion. "That's it!" she replied. "Thank you, very much Millie" I answered mechanically, as I hung up the phone.

The amazing constant in all of these stories of betrayal is that the offending party couldn't stand to be cheated on. It was their greatest fear. This is a trait that afflicts both men and women. They don't allow you to enjoy the same benefits that they feel they're entitled. Secondly, they use the guise of their love against you. Let's be honest. People couldn't get nearly as much out of you as they do; if they didn't profess to love you.

My mother once told me that true love will make you feel a lot of things, but pain shouldn't be one of them. I know there is a special place in hell for those who unnecessarily break the hearts of others, but my sincere hope is that none of the special women I've encountered in my life has a reservation.

# Chapter Fifty

## Answers

The unfortunate reality about relationships is that most people don't understand the basic premise or purpose; the goal is happiness for your partner. Without this basic understanding people enter into countless encounters seeking their own happiness. That approach never works. Why? It has singular focus. All the energy of one person is being devoted to the satisfaction of one person, you.

Consider this: people may have several reasons for why they are initially attracted to you, but only one reason why they will stay. That reason is simple, they stay because of the way you make **them feel**. Therefore to build a successful relationship, the focus should be on the other person. Everyone likes to think that they are important to someone. It is fundamental: primal. So if an outing is planned with the other person is mind, even if it doesn't turn out as well as you planned. The satisfaction will come from the fact that the thought and intention of the outing was their happiness. People often rate the quality of the relationship based on what they get out of it. These people are guilty of reverse thinking. That is, they put the result ahead of the input. When given the opportunity I always ask these people the following question: What do you think your partner got out of the relationship? It usually stumps them.

When I hear people say that relationships "should be 50/50" or a case of "give and take", I chuckle. Both of these premises are fundamentally flawed. The first, intimates that effort and production should be equal. The second proposes a selfish philosophy that suggests "quid pro quo" (something given for something gained). These trains of thought are both on tracks that lead to nothing but disappointment and animosity. I prefer to think of relationships as give and receive. Why? People rarely have the same emotional or physical requirements of a relationship. So why should they have the same input? If Partner A **gives** Partner B all the emotional/mental/physical stimulation they require to make them happy, they are

better equipped and therefore more likely to **give** the same requirements to Partner A in return. Not the same actions, the necessary
requirements. The result is a perpetual motion machine, self contained, harmonious and stable._

A 50/50 relationship hints at the concept of holding back, not doing
more than you have to or worse, not more than your partner. Do
you think it is more prudent to expend all of your energy to pro-
duce a result that brings very little joy to your partner or, use less
than half of your energy to deliver exactly what he or she desires.
Conversely, the concept of 50/50 incorrectly attempts to measure
the wrong thing. Its focus is perceived input into the relationship.
Remember, the goal is **mutual** happiness. Nothing else matters.

Many of you may have friends that easily get first dates, but not
many second ones. Perhaps you know someone that been engaged
several times, but never married. The reason is the same. They
have the bait to hook them, but they can't "close the deal". Let's
use physical attractiveness as an example because it is an easy
concept for everyone to relate to, and therefore understand. A man
may ask a woman out on a date because she is attractive to him, he
thinks. The real reason is how he thinks **he will feel** if she accepts
his invitation and agrees to be seen in public with him. That feeling is shattered however, if while on the date the woman flirts with
other men in the room. The same thing applies to women when
men's eyes wander. People can't "close the deal" because they
either lose focus and their partner doesn't "feel special" anymore,
or they lack the substance and depth to maintain a fruitful relationship.

In a perfect world, all post pubescent individuals would undergo
emotional sensitivity training before taking a relationship Hippo-
cratic Oath. That's correct, a lifelong pledge to do no intentional
physical, emotional or mental harm to relationship partners. A
clear statement of intent would have to presented and agreed upon
before the relationship could proceed. When the stated goal is
reached or if it is determined that there is little to no hope of mutual satisfaction, the contract would be amicably dissolved. Keep
in mind. There is nothing wrong with any type of relationship that
is mutually agreed upon. I propose this concept in jest of course.

However, nothing is more evil and hurtful than to deceive someone in the name of love.

In the final analysis, I urge you take the plunge. Embrace the possibilities of love, its ups and its downs; the joy and the pain. Love and let someone love you in return. Take the exhilarating ride that is truly a blessing that has been bestowed only on humans. Grow and benefit from the exchange of ideas, emotions, experiences (not to mention bodily fluids) that only occurs in an intimate relationship. Feel the joy and sense of accomplishment that comes from making someone else happy! Humankind was not meant to be alone; your life is not all about you. It was meant to be shared by two! Despite all the sadness and pain that I have endured; I would not trade one minute of the good times to erase years of the bad. "Live your life such that memory loss would be a tragedy." I challenge you. Take charge, take a chance, and make your move. Only trees have to live where they're planted, rooted and bound to current circumstance. Nonetheless; even they bask in the sun, soak in the rain. They provide shade and shelter to those who seek them. Cruel carvings hurt them now and again, but over time they heal and serve as lasting tributes to love now gone. Swaying in the winds of change, they sometimes lose a valuable piece of their structure, but still they survive. Strengthening and growing during the good times, while dropping their leaves in dormancy, during the harsh cold. Still, deep in the roots that bind them to the earth remains their indomitable spirit; a vow that when the warmth returns to try once again.

All relationships end eventually; some crash land after a long adventure (death). Others are incinerated upon re-entry (circumstance). Then there are those that die before they have a chance to blossom. They are the ones that haunt you with what could have been, and what might have happened. This tribute is for a participant in one of those circumstances.

## The Face of an Angel

### A Tribute to Carolyn

She possessed skin so lovely, whether tanned or made up. Beauty delicately stretched over a gentile frame. She was always kind and accessible; though I didn't know her name. Emotions lay obvious for everyone to see. A warm, engaging smile combined with cheeks of just the right color, obvious proof that her beauty was more than skin deep. Dark wind-blown hair provided a varying frame, to a look far greater than the sum of its parts. To find the source of her power; the center of grace, you merely have to gaze upon her face. Marvel at the rare jewels she calls eyes, dark, rich and character filled. To look into them is to dive in head first, only then can you experience their amazing depth, find your true worth. Wide as the universe; as deep as the sea, her eyes are the source of the beauty we see. Contained in those wondrous orbs is the comfort that knowledge and compassion brings. They are an endless source of warmth that highlights her face. Backlit by a galaxy of stars, excitement and enthusiasm are always there for the asking. Whether serious as a judge, sparkling or shedding tears; her eyes are brilliant yet constant standards, belying her years. I can only imagine them in the light of a candle or dare I say, in white hot passion. Either way they are truly an example of the best that God can fashion.

Written in reverence and admiration of my new friend, Carolyn.

Thank You,

James Robert Russell

# Chapter Fifty-Two

## The Sea

The sea: endless, boundless, stretching as far as the eye can see. Voluminous: its swirling blue-green currents always in motion, spanning the horizon. Rising and falling, ebb and flow. Lifetime journey, a dependable constant, full of life, capable of death. Mirror of sunlight, harbinger of storms. Boundless, containing amazing aspirations along with dashed hopes and shattered dreams. Calmness in its surface; soothing serenity in its sound. Confidence and hope spawned by the relentless work of its waves. White capped crests followed by deep troughs. Varying wavelengths; the heartbeat of the sea. Constant energy nourishing the planet, every view seems personal and private, but it's emotion and inspiration are obviously plain for all to see.

Every sunrise and sunset, a horizontal tapestry unfurls, air brush and watercolors blend whimsical thoughts and concrete plans. Sunlight for fuel, starlight to dream. Varying sky tones blue-white to blue-black. The sea in its vastness represents dreams and hopes to some, to others only hopelessness and despair. Possessing the ability to deliver both soothing words and pleasure or spirit crushing barbs and pain.

The ebb and flow of the tide affected by external forces, mirroring the give and take of cohabitation. The constant exchange of energy, waves to the shore. Support and acceptance, an endless cycle. Erosion in some places, deposits in others. Calm surface hides strong currents beneath. From seemingly nowhere the violent storm erupts; it's fury mimics passion. The sea, like a lover has countless secrets hidden in its depths. Buried treasure or certain destruction. The sea, necessary for human survival, providing both nourishment and enjoyment. Ageless, timeless and indestructible. Equaled only by love, marriage and devotion.

# Chapter Fifty-Three

## Epilogue

My life has always been an open book. An epic novel of a life well lived; not perfect mind you, but enjoyed nonetheless. It's the story of a man and his emotions, his intensity and pain. A tale of adventure, romance, comedy and tragedy all rolled into one. It has been documented in all of its gory and glorious details, a recipe for a sumptuous meal that I hope you've enjoyed. It is important because it details the life of a very human being. No more or less important than any other, but documented in a way that hopefully has caused its readers to the take time to evaluate their own lives and their effect on others that have crossed their path. It is potentially a golden opportunity to revisit and analyze past problems, hidden haunts of long ago. Hopefully, it has been a look into the crystal ball, revealing a treasure map to the riches of love in the future. Personally, at a minimum it has been a cleansing, a release of some of the pain. The most important thing to take from this is the magnitude of love that has been exchanged. This writing is both a celebration of and a tribute to the characters that have been detailed within. I may have been blessed with the tremendous ability to remember incidents in my life in incredible detail. But I could not have done it unless the subjects weren't as memorable as the wonderful women I have been blessed to encounter.

My experiences: ranging from being beaten-up because I liked a girl, to being beaten-up by a girl because I didn't like her. Participation in scenes of passion ranging from a lover running barefoot in a bathrobe in the driving rain to beg for forgiveness and another chance; to another throwing her wedding rings over a cliff to prove her devotion. Not to mention spontaneous and sometimes very public love scenes that would rival anything Hollywood has ever produced. Poignant memories of first kisses, amazing orgasms and the joy of shared laugher to the painful sound of a lover's door closing for the last time. From the preacher's words "you may kiss the bride" to the sound of the judge's gavel and "it is so ordered."

The romantic moments contrasted with the pain of tearful replays of acts of infidelity, shattered dreams and blatant lies, all taking place in some beautiful, exotic and unexpected places gives me cause for pause, yet hope for tomorrow in this hopefully unfinished classic.

It is my life and I am happy with it, yet admittedly on occasion I am saddened by it. But most importantly, it is life and it beats the hell out of anything finishing second.

Thank you so very much for sharing my life. Comments and questions are welcome and encouraged. Please visit me @ deliciousrejection.com